I DID THAT!

John Cathro Seed, M.D.

Illustrations: Ralph Schlegel

Drawings: Ralph Schlegel

Published by   Paradigma Ltd.
                    Internet: www.paradigma-publishing.com
                    e-mail: info@paradigma-publishing.com

ISBN 978-1-906833-06-0

Contents

Acknowledgements:

Victoria Adams, Kristine and Ryan Persichilli

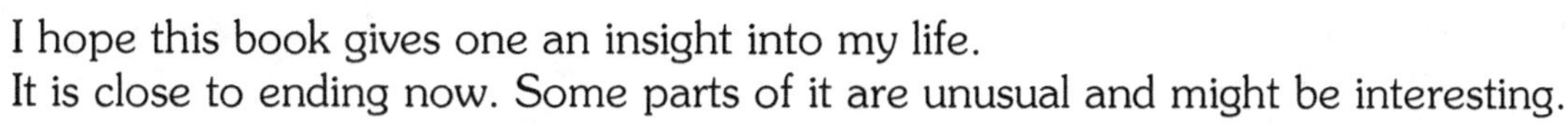

I hope this book gives one an insight into my life.
It is close to ending now. Some parts of it are unusual and might be interesting.

Helping People Die

In the late 1950's I was working at Memorial Sloan-Kettering Institute when a colleague mentioned an unusual nursing facility called the Calvary House that catered to the terminally ill poor. I was intrigued by the concept and stopped by to visit the facility. My first observation on the ward was a patient screaming: "I'm dying, I'm dying! I don't want to die!" The patient was suffering from advanced leukemia (a cancer), and back in those days there was little hope for people with advanced stages of cancer (much has changed for the better since then). So there was little denying that she was correct, she was going to die. But I thought "That's one hell of a way to die." That episode had a tremendous effect on me. I made arrangements to help out at the facility and from then on, every time I saw a patient, I was thinking about what could be done to prevent the fear of dying. That's not a trivial task by any means since most people have a (relatively healthy) fear of dying. In the terminally ill person it's counterproductive and unnecessary. The critical point is that the dying person should look forward to going comfortably to death. Everything is taken care of, there is no pain and there is nothing more to be done. That is pretty much the standard of care now, but in the 1950's it was rare and not widely appreciated. So there was little structure and next to no support for this approach to caring for the terminally ill.

In order to be successful, I had to have the complete confidence of the patients that I would be there to help them whenever they needed it. So if they asked to see me, I always saw them that day. Whatever the problem was, I always had something encouraging to say that day and would follow up the next day. My attitude was that something ought to help their symptoms or problem. Even if there was no immediate remedy, maybe we could find the answer in the next day or two. I was always pleasant, never looked worried and saw the patients frequently. I made a point of laughing or joking with them on occasion. I treated the employees who made their beds and cleaned them or fed them (if necessary) with courtesy and professionalism, and took care to listen to their concerns as well. As a result, the atmosphere in the facility was positive and supportive; the patients had confidence in me and I was always around to tend to their needs. One time I came to see two women who were in beds next to each other. There was a nurse there to wash the patients, change their sheets and perform whatever routine tasks were necessary to get the patients ready for the day. I waited for the nurse to finish her task. While I was waiting, and after the nurse had finished with the second patient, she turned back to the first patient only to find that she had just died. After confirming with me that the first patient had died, she turned back to the second patient, only to find that she had just died as well. The nurse choked up a bit while I was there, so I focused my attention on the nurse and helped her to grieve over the death of her patients.

While I was as helpful and cheerful as I could be, I was also very frank and informative. If the patient said, "I think I am going to die tonight", the proper answer was, "Yes, you may". If the patient was worrying and wondering about the possibility that I might have overlooked something that would delay his or her death, they immediately would tell what it is that bothered them. I would ask questions and do a physical exam if warranted, reassuring them that there was nothing more to do. Ninety percent of the time they were right. Some patients, knowing all about their problem, look forward to dying.

One time I had a male patient who frequently complained, "Why hasn't the Lord taken me yet?" I would tell him, "I don't think He is up to it yet", or I might say, "Maybe He thinks you ought to put in more time on life", or "Are you sure you have everything ready?" "Maybe He is too busy." "Ask Him (teasing) next week." Then one evening, the Irish man said to me, "I think I am going to die tonight." I said, "I think you will die tonight and I will pray for you." He replied, "I will pray for you too, Doc." That night he died.

I had a Catholic Jesuit Priest who was my patient. He had cancer and he wanted to know the course of his disease. I pointed out that there are five different routes that patients have with his disease. During the next six or seven days I told him in detail about all five routes. There was no big rush. Everyday in the Calvary Hospital I would see him and talk to him. I asked him how he felt and talked about the details, if he wanted. After a couple of weeks, he recognized that he was leaning towards one of the five routes. He asked me if he was in group number three. I said, "Yes". After that we did not talk at all about his disease. We talked about anything that was happening in football games and other sports. One day, after two or three months of talking to him, he recognized that he was getting worse. I told him that he would die in the next day or two. I shook his hand and said, "I feel honored for having taken care of you." He died that night.

A woman who had cancer in the neck came in with her husband. She was comfortable and her husband was going to come back to see her in two days. Before he left I took him over to the nurse's site and explained to him just what would happen and how it would happen. I told him that cancer growing in the neck on the carotid artery is apt to grow into the artery, weakening the wall of the artery and eventually breaking the artery. This usually causes a big flow of blood upward going up two or three feet. The flow would end in about nine seconds and then the heart would stop. A large towel to collect the flow is kept near the patient's neck. Unbeknown to us he came in the following day to see his wife. While he was sitting at her side she had a blow out. Everything was going as I had predicted, yet he was not afraid. He took her hand as she died, and I arrived around fifteen minutes later. When it was all over he thanked me for having told him ahead of time what would happen.

One time we had a very difficult patient who had an uncanny ability to make people angry. No matter what other people did, she always managed to insult them. She constantly complained about what they did, always criticizing them and swearing at them. One could not say something nice to her without being shouted at and insulted for it. She had to be fed and even be put on a bed pan for urinating. She swore at everyone that helped her, therefore nobody wanted to. My solution was to give her medication to subdue her to the point where she could not talk and it worked.

Another time we had a patient with an opening in the stomach that went into the wall of the intestines. The hole was so large that it opened up on the wall of the abdomen. When she ate acidic foods with enzymes to digest the food, it would also digest part of the wall of the abdomen. Cleaning up the wall was hard to do, so what we did was pharmacologically shut down the walls of the intestine. Then when it was time to feed the patient three nurses stood by and kept the food in the intestine and kept the skin from being dissolved. That lasted three weeks.

Although I was making progress in improving the treatment of terminally ill cancer patients and reducing the fear of death, the nursing facility was struggling to keep its doors open. They were having a hard time getting the money to keep the program going for the poor cancer patients. I suggested that if we converted the nursing home into a hospital, we wouldn't have trouble financing it, because welfare would pay for it. The sister in charge approved and gave me permission to go ahead and make it into a hospital.

Making a Hospital

The first step in transforming Calvary House into a hospital was to hire two physicians to work part time. One was an attending physician in gastroenterology at Cornell Hospital in the Manhattan section of New York City. He also continued to work on research in the field of gastroenterology. The other physician was an attending internal medicine physician at Albert Einstein Hospital in the Bronx. I was a member of the Social Sciences Department of the Albert Einstein Medical School for fifteen years. We hired a pathologist who came every Tuesday afternoon and did an autopsy on whoever died that day or the day before.

We needed to have a laboratory and that would require regulatory approval and a director. The laboratory that we already had was a good one. I thought I could be the Laboratory Director, so I applied to the New York City Department of Health for a permit to run a laboratory. They sent out a woman to interview me. When she looked at what I did in the laboratory and how I kept and distributed the records, she was very impressed. I analyzed the data with a time series technique, a statistical technique that was seldom in use at that time. The following day after the interview, I was given a permit to run a hospital laboratory. I was permitted to be the director of any hospital laboratory in New York City (Cornell, Columbia, New York, etc). The final step was to

get the hospital approved by the Joint Commission for inspecting hospitals. When they got through their inspection they said, "Calvary Hospital is the best run hospital we have ever inspected." We were fully accredited. It also made an impression on the Cardinal who had a lot of hospitals under his care in his Diocese, and Calvary was the best of them all.

Gold Medal

We changed Calvary Home to Calvary Hospital in 1962. When it was complete we decided to send invitations for a ceremony dedicating the new wing to Cardinal Spellman. On the day of the dedication there was a little platform and a number of chairs. All the important Catholic people in Manhattan attended, as well as well known priests from other areas. During the ceremonies, there were fifteen minutes scheduled for Cardinal Spellman to speak. When his time came, he went up on the platform and signaled for me to come up. I didn't come up, but when he insisted I went up. When I got up he gave the signal to another man to come up on the stage, who then pinned a gold medal, the Pro Ecclesia et Pontifice Cross on my jacket. Afterwards, there was applause from the audience. I talked about the achievements at Calvary, what we were doing, and what we planned to do. After the official ceremonies were over, the Cardinal sat down and invited my children, who were small, to sit on his lap. It caught me totally by surprise; I never thought something like that might happen. In addition to the gold medal, I was also given a document signed by Pope John the 23rd, acknowledging the award, which is given two or three times a year in the Catholic Papacy.

Following the solemn dedication of the newly reconstructed House of Calvary in the Bronx, His Eminence Francis Cardinal Spellman pauses with Sister M. Gemma, administrator, second from left, as the Rt. Rev. Msgr. George H. Guilfoyle, executive director of Catholic Charities, left, and Mother Rose Xavier, Mother General of the Dominican Sisters of the Sick Poor who staff the hospital, look on. (Dowling Photo)

The Cardinal Blesses the House of Calvary

Cardinal Spellman, above, blesses the interior of newly reconstructed House of Calvary Hospital. Assisting His Eminence are the Rt. Rev. Msgr. James B. Nash, left, and the Rt. Rev. Msgr. John M. Brew. The Rev. Christopher J. Kane, assistant director of the Health and Hospitals Department of New York Catholic Charities, stands on at the left. (Dowling Photo)

Cardinal Blesses House of Calvary

Msgr. Guilfoyle Reviews Contributions Made By Sisters and Volunteers in His Talk

A dedication gift of $50,000 from the estate of the late Mrs. Mary E. Welsh was bestowed by Francis Cardinal Spellman on the House of Calvary during ceremonies marking the completion of the newly reconstructed hospital at 1600 Macombs Road, Bronx, on Saturday, July 23. His Eminence presented this check to Mother Rose Xavier, Mother General of the Dominican Sisters of the Sick Poor. The Cardinal also announced a legacy of $70,000 due August 1 from the estate of the late Mrs. Sarah Smith. Mrs. Smith was one of the original 12 women of Calvary who, under the leadership of the late Mrs. Catherine McParlan, founded the House of Calvary in 1899. The $120,000 total will be applied towards the $1,135,000 cost for modernization of the hospital plant initiated in 1960.

Assisting his Eminence in the blessing of the interior of the hospital were the Rt. Rev. Msgr. Owen J. Scanlan as assistant priest and the Rt. Rev. Monsignori James B. Nash and John M. Brew as deacons of honor. The Rt. Rev. Msgr. Patrick V. Ahearn, the Very Rev. Msgr. Patrick J. Frawley and the Rev. Christopher G. Kane were masters of ceremonies. Members of the Knights of Columbus and a group of Xavier High School students formed an honor guard at the ceremonies and music was provided by the Dominican Sisters of the Sick Poor.

Dr. Seed Honored

At the outdoor civic ceremonies which followed, Cardinal Spellman presented Dr. John Cathro Seed, medical director of the hospital, with the Pro Ecclesia et Pontifice Cross, papal award for outstanding service to the Church and Pontiff, stating it was a symbol of "our gratitude for all that you do for all of us. Only God could inspire such service as you have given to the patients here."

His Eminence also paid tribute to the dedicated lives of the Dominican Sisters of the Sick Poor who staff the hospital and said that for many souls the House of Calvary is a gate of Heaven.

chronicled the development of the hospital by recalling the three groups of dedicated women who contributed to its growth: Mrs. Catherine McParlan and the Women of Calvary who founded in 1899, the Dominican Sisters of Blauvelt who staffed it from 1910 to 1958 and the Dominican Sisters of the Sick Poor who now operate the hospital.

Tributes Paid

He paid tribute to Mrs. McParlan, a childless widow, who became the dynamic nucleus of 12 widows, calling themselves the Women of Calvary, whose self-sacrificing lives made possible the first House of Calvary at Perry Street in Greenwich Village for the care of poverty-stricken and incurable cancer victims.

"Mrs. McParlan died on January 29, 1958, at the venerable age of 102," he recounted. "To her as the last survivor of the original 12 Women of Calvary is due the gratitude of over 15,000 men and women of every race, creed and color. Without her 'charity, humility, sacrifice and prayer' — the motto engraved on her cross of acceptance as a Woman of Calvary — their haven in sickness and death might never have survived."

The Dominican Sisters of Blauvelt, he said, also merited special tribute for their devoted and selfless service to cancer patients during the 40 year period in the House of Calvary's history, dating from 1918 to 1958. Because of their many other missions and their growing responsibilities in the field of education, these Sisters requested and were granted permission to be replaced at the hospital in order to concentrate on their other works, Monsignor Guilfoyle explained. He paid them reverent tribute for all they have meant to the Home and Hospital and to the Archdiocese of New York.

Dominicans' History

Monsignor Guilfoyle then traced the history of the hospital's present staff of Sisters, the Dominican Sisters of the Sick Poor, founded as a religious order of visiting nurse Sisters by an Irish immigrant

Cardinal Blesses Houses of Calvary

Director Receives Papal Honor
(Printed from the Catholic News, June 30th, 1962)

At the outdoor civic ceremonies which followed, Cardinal Spellman presented Dr. John Cathro Seed, medical director of the hospital, with the **Pro Ecclesia et Pontifice Cross**, papal award for outstanding service to the Church and Pontiff, stating it was a symbol of "our gratitude for all that you do for all of us. Only God could inspire such service as you have given to the patients here."

By-Laws and Corruption

Among the many issues I was required to deal with in making the transition from a nursing facility to a hospital was a new set of By Laws that specified how the facility was to be run. They included specifications on how doctors were hired by the hospital and what qualifications needed to be. Unfortunately, shortly after the conversion to a hospital, a dispute erupted between myself and the Sister who was in charge of the hospital. She told one of the other doctors that his brother could be on the medical staff. However, in doing so she did not follow the By-Laws. I told her that we would have to follow the By-Laws in hiring the new doctor. It was a difficult argument, but she ultimately was forced to acknowledge that she had not followed the By Laws and was obligated to do so. Perhaps not surprisingly, when we followed the rules on physician hiring in the By-Laws, the brother was not offered the position. The following day the Sister told me that I would no longer be allowed to do research. Since virtually all of the changes and improvements to patient care were result of my research, I felt obligated to resign and did so the following day. I turned in my resignation the next day. It was accepted.

So I left Calvary Hospital. I attempted to perpetuate my approach to patient care by leaving a complete set of written instructions, but that was destined to failure. A year later, most of the procedures and approaches to patient care that I had developed had been abandoned. At the time I left, all the major hospitals in New York City were sending difficult patients to Calvary Hospital. Ten years later that was no longer the case. It made me feel very sad, all these people not getting the treatment they could get.

The Seeds and Cathros

I was born at the Saint Mary Hospital in Rochester, Minnesota on February 26, 1922. At that time my father was a resident at the Mayo Clinic in Rochester, Minnesota. In the spring of 1924, my mother was sitting on a bench with me in a carriage and next to us was another mother with her child in a carriage of about the same age. After awhile my mother noticed that I was orange colored compared to the other woman's son, so she rushed me into the clinic thinking I was jaundiced, which is a sign of liver damage. Instead, it was Carotenemia. The orange skin discoloration was due to the body absorbing the orange color from carrots and it being deposited in the skin cells. My mother knew that carrots were good for babies and were among the only foods I did not resist eating, so she fed me a lot of carrots and consequently I absorbed their orange color.

Kindergarten

When I was in kindergarten I didn't like the other children. One time, I knocked out the front teeth of another boy. My father strapped me 5 times with his belt across the bottom as punishment. As a result, I could not sit down for two days. As time went on, I still didn't get along with the other children. When they came near the sandbox, I would throw sand at them. I was soon advised that I shouldn't do that. So, wherever the other children were together playing during the morning recess, I would move far away. I would refuse to see or play with any of them.

The Ice Man

One day I decided to join the iceman to avoid school. I would sit in the seat next to him. They didn't have refrigerators in those days, instead they had ice boxes. The ice man would go into the alleys between the houses on a horse-drawn carriage delivering ice to the people along the way. I knew where he would be on his route. I would leave the house at that time so I could join him and sit up front with him. When school was over, I would get home at the same time as the other children. This went on for about ten days, until one day my mother went to the grocery store and my kindergarten teacher happened to be there at the same time. She asked my mother, "How's little Johnny?" My mother said, "Why do you ask?" The teacher said, "He hasn't been in school for the last ten days. I assumed that he has been sick." My mother advised her that I had left for school every day and that I came home on time. When I got home that day, the truth came out that I had been spending the time with the iceman. I was admonished for that, but at least I did not get strapped. Apparently my parents thought it was a pretty ingenious way to avoid school. Nevertheless, they advised me to go to school and not to join the iceman and I did so without further protest.

At the end of the first year, my teacher thought that I should stay another year in kindergarten and learn how to be social with the other children. I had flunked kindergarten. My mother protested and pleaded that I be let into the first grade. The school finally gave in and allowed me to proceed into first grade. The first grade teacher said, "He doesn't belong here. "You should put him in second grade." So, they put me in second grade, I settled down and things went very well.

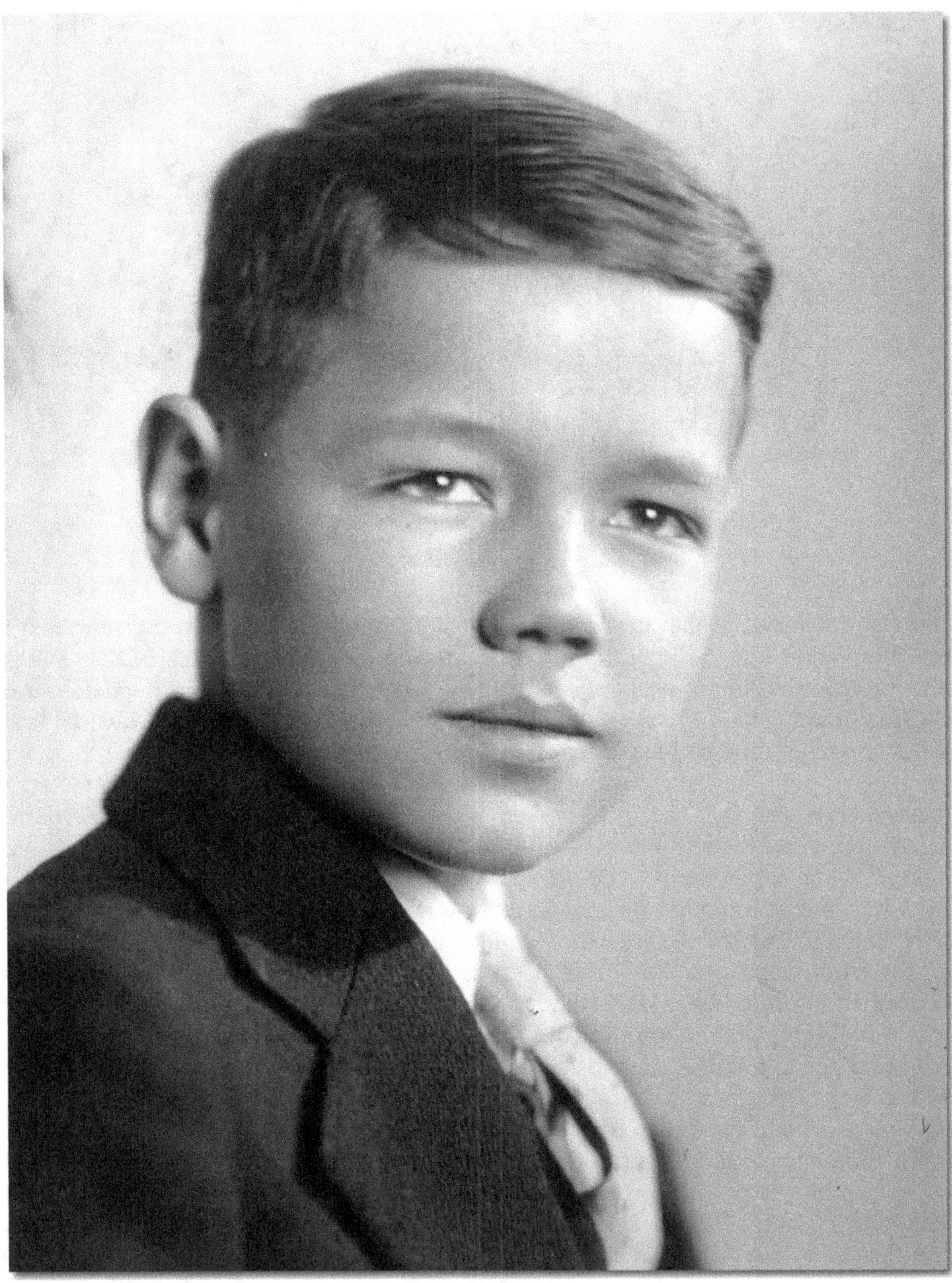

Snow Pile

My sister, Linda, and I were on our way to school one morning after a snow storm, and there was a snow pile on the sidewalk. I jumped over it, but Linda couldn't jump over the snow. I told her to go back home, so she went back home. When I came back home from school my father strapped me yet again, this time for not helping my sister get across the snow pile. I never liked my sister very much after that.

Five Years Old & the Phone Rang

One time, when I was five years old, my parents left me alone in the house with my sister. The phone rang and when I answered it, it was a Polish man. I could not understand anything that he said. I didn't get his name or phone number. When my father came home, I told him a man called, but I could not understand what he was saying. Three hours later the man called again and that time my father got the message. The man had appendicitis and my father went to the hospital and operated on him. The man survived. When my father came home, he gave me a strong lashing for not getting his phone number. From that point on I hated telephone calls. Whenever a telephone rang, it made my heart beat fast for about three to five minutes. I finally got over that apprehension about telephones and the ringing when I was about fifty years old.

Elmer

My grades in elementary school were not very good. They were passing, but my parents felt that I could do a lot better. There was another student in the class named Elmer who was the son of one of the teachers. His grades were better than mine and my parents constantly reminded me of this fact. However, I did not care about getting good grades and cared even less about how Elmer was doing.

In seventh grade, we were expected to learn about the library. I became interested in the first Bible ever printed by Johannes Gutenberg in 1450. To learn how to do research on finding this Bible, I went to our neighbor, who lived two houses down and who was in charge of the John Creare Technical Library, located in downtown Chicago. I went to his library five or six times. He taught me how to find my way around the library. I took out books, and read everything I could about the Gutenberg press, and then made a model of it out of matchsticks for my science project. No one else came close to doing what I did. I gained the ability and skill to find things in the library! Elmer's project was by far inferior and I never heard about him again.

Fast Growing In High School

At the beginning of high school, all the boys had their heights measured. I was fourth from the smallest. During that year, my clothes were shrinking rapidly. My mother went from store to store to complain about their fabrics. She told them that after she washed my shirts once or twice, they would shrink an inch or two and they were becoming too small for me. The salesman would apologize, but there was nothing they could do about it. The following year in school we were all measured again and I was now the tallest of the five hundred boys in my class. I had grown over a foot in that year. My mother went around to the stores again, this time apologizing to the sales people. It wasn't their clothes, it was me!

He Hasn't Done A Bit of Homework

In high school boys learned tradecrafts such as making furniture, operating printing presses, and soldering metals among others. In my freshman class in high school, I made the desk that I used at home. I really enjoyed making things, but there was another thing about this class that made it enjoyable; there wasn't any homework! I managed to stay in the top ten percent in high school without doing much homework. I got enough done in the ten minutes between classes to make a reasonable showing. My French teacher, in particular, gave me a hard time about not spending more time learning French. Finally, my father took me into the principal's office at the beginning of the third year of high school. My father said, "He hasn't done a bit of homework in the last two years. He has to learn to do homework somewhere. Could you give him an extra academic course?" The principal said, "Okay, he has to learn German in addition to French and his other courses." My grades improved.

She Would Blush

After my father talked with the principal, I was taking one more class than all the other students. I liked that, but I still hated the French teacher. So I decided to really learn French so I could embarrass her. She was not a native Parisian and I thought that she might make minor mistakes in translating. I read an additional 3,000 pages in French, on my own, outside of the regularly assigned work. She would give assignments of two pages to read after which she would ask the class if they had any questions. I would raise my hand if I thought she had made a minor error. I would give my translation and she would blush and become flustered.

As the years went by she forgot what a nasty student I was and encouraged other students to read more French outside of the class "just like I did". This created a problem for my sister and brothers, who were forced to endure constant reminders. "Your brother read 3,000 pages of French outside of class, why don't you read some extra French?" Needless to say, they did not enjoy the constant reminders. It's probably best that they didn't know why I had been such a prolific reader!

Number One

By having an extra course, I had so much work that I couldn't complete it in the time between classes in order to get good grades. So I figured if I had to do some homework, I might as well do all the homework and do more work than was required. My grades shot up, instead of being in the top ten percent, I was number one in a class of a thousand. One day my trigonometry teacher put a problem up on the board. He said, "I think this problem can be solved, but I've never seen it solved." It took me until three o'clock in the morning, but the following day I came to class and showed him and my classmates how I got the answer.

During my last two years in high school, I was on my school's tennis team and swimming team. The tennis team used to be the ball runners for the National Clay Tennis Matches. The world champions played in these matches. It was a thrill to be helping them and to be able to talk to them. For the swim team, I swam backstroke. At the end of the season, there was always a match between us and the team from New Trier. The swimmer who swam backstroke from New Trier used a different technique than all the other backstroke swimmers for almost a year. After learning of it, we were trying to use it too. This was a regular standard race but there were six people timing it because the top swimmers were expected to beat the world record; they did. The first three all shattered the existing record. I was the fifth out of the field of six, but felt honored to have been in the race. After all, we were only high school students and yet we were breaking world records.

There were two things I remembered in my senior year. In English class, there was a competition to see who could memorize the longest poem. Each student stood up and recited his or her poem without an error. I came in second with the following poem choice:

Elegy Written in a Country Church-yard
By Thomas Gray

The curfew tolls the knell of parting day,
The lowing herd winds slowly o'er the lea,
The ploughman homeward plods his weary way,
And leaves the world to darkness and to me.

Now fades the glimmering landscape on the sight,
And all the air a solemn stillness holds,
Save where the beetle wheels his droning flight,
And drowsy tinklings lull the distant folds:

Save that from yonder ivy-mantled tower
The moping owl does to the moon complain
Of such as, wandering near her secret bower,
Molest her ancient solitary reign.

Beneath those rugged elms, that yew-tree's shade,
Where heaves the turf in many a mouldering heap,
Each in his narrow cell for ever laid,
The rude Forefathers of the hamlet sleep.
(Continuing on for a total of 116 lines)

The man who beat me chose the following poem:

The Rime of the Ancient Mariner
By Samuel Taylor Coleridge

It is an ancient Mariner,
And he stoppeth one of three,
The Rime of the Ancient Mariner
"By thy long grey beard and glittering eye,
Now wherefore stopp'st thou me?
(Continuing on for a total 126 lines)

Boy Scouts

While in Boy Scouts I had to mount three animals for my taxidermy merit badge. One was a sparrow, the other a mouse and I don't remember what the third one was for sure, but I believe it was a rabbit. We would take out the guts and stuff the animals so that they looked alive. One day during my senior year of high school, my mother was holding a very elegant luncheon. Before I went to school that morning I left my stuffed mouse on the floor, just behind the front left leg of one of the chairs in the living room. My mouse had nice black eyes peaking around the corner of the chair leg. Midway through the luncheon, a woman screamed "There's a mouse! There's a mouse!" There were about twelve or fifteen women, and they all scattered away from the chair. My mother came in, picked up the mouse and exclaimed, "That son of mine!"

I heard about it that evening when my father arrived home. I took back my mouse and put it with my other mounted creatures. When I came back from college for Christmas, the first thing I did was look for my mouse. My mouse was gone! My mother had thrown it out, without my permission. It was a shame, since it had been the perfect mouse; it looked just like a live one, with the fur and the eyes. I learned that mothers don't appreciate the beauty of mice.

For the astronomy merit badge we had to plot the course of the planets for six months. One was required to make a copy of the constellations visible and then show where the planets were moving among the constellations. The map I made was given to a forty year old amateur astronomer who lived in the neighborhood. He would test me on my knowledge for the Boy Scouts. I passed! Eventually, I obtained a merit badge for all the nature study badges and became an Eagle Scout with ten extra merit badges than required. During the summer before I damaged my left foot, I was an instructor at the Boy Scouts summer camp south of Muskegon, Michigan on the eastern side of Lake Michigan. It was the same camp that I had gone to when I was seven years old. There was singing around a campfire and story telling. On top of a dune near the edge of the lake, there was a large sparse tree. At its top, about thirty feet from the ground, there was a huge eagle's nest measuring at least four feet across. It was something to see the eagles come and go to feed their young.

One evening around 10:00 pm, when I was a sixteen year old Boy Scout, I was walking with a friend along the beach. There was a fairly good breeze that evening and the waves were about two feet high. While walking along we saw a distress flare from a sailboat, which was competing in the Chicago to Mackinac sailboat race. The boat was about two hundred yards from the shore. We went back to the camp where we were staying and we got a canoe. We then tried to go out and help them, but as we were paddling our canoe would fill up with water. We would have to jump out, empty the canoe, and climb back in continuously. We got within about seventy yards of the boat when the Coast Guard finally arrived. We then turned around back towards the shore.

A Summer to Remember

The summer before my third year of high school, I went on a Boy Scout camping trip with five boys and a father of one of the boys. The six of us were driven across Sault St. Marie into Canada and into the town of Hayden. We then went from there to our starting point, a small town in Canada north of Hayden and near to Lake Michigan, only reachable by a train. The day the train left there were no passenger cars available, so they set us up in an empty freight car. The middle of the freight car had an open door in which we could sit with our legs bent out of the car. The train traveled at about 25 miles per hour. With slingshots we shot rocks at telephone polls along the path. We got out of the train at an isolated town near our starting point and we took two taxies to the lake. We took out our kayaks and put them in the water and proceeded to cross the lake to where we put up our tents for the night.

While eating we became aware of a buzzing noise off in the distance. We heard a constant buzzing sound all night long. We went inside the tent and we couldn't figure out what exactly it was. We soon learned it was the buzzing of mosquitoes! Gradually the noise became louder and louder, there were so many mosquitoes making so much noise, it was as if an airplane was flying right overhead. During the day, the mosquitoes were back in the woods, but as the sun went down, they came out. After a while there were so many mosquitoes that we could not see the camp fire outside because the mosquitoes were settled on the netting. If we touched the tents we could briefly see the fire. Within five or six seconds the mosquitoes would come back. If inside the netting you were safe, but if you stepped outside they would bite.

The next day we took a route that crossed through three lakes. On the far side of the third lake we saw from a distance what looked like an animal. When we came closer, we saw that it was a dead Bull Moose that was approximately 1,200 pounds. The moose's hind leg was missing, and there were huge black marks on it. A grizzly bear probably killed the moose within the last day. It was getting to be noon time and there was a trail leading to the river, which was the rest of our path. We didn't know how long it was and we were worried about meeting the grizzly bear along the way. A stream of water on the trail would lead us to a river that would take us to a big lake. This would be our ending point. We were thinking that the walk to this river might not help us avoid the grizzly, being as tired as we were after the lake. We decided to stay near to where the dead moose was found. We took out our kayaks and paddled across the lake. We were a little bit anxious that evening about being eaten ourselves. We hoped that the bear wouldn't want us. We gathered enough wood to feed the fire all night with five foot long logs. We made a pile three feet high and thirty feet long because we knew that wild animals were afraid of fire. There were six of us, so we worked in pairs of two. If one fellow got drowsy, the other would stay up and keep the fire going strong. When we got up the next day we quickly left the area, hoping we wouldn't see or hear the grizzly bear! We would be at the river and eventually the river.

Bang!

We got to a river and then put our boats in it. We thought we had enough food, but the energy that it took to row for that long was more than what our food supply could replenish. There were plenty of pike that had grown to about two and a half to three feet long. We hadn't planned on doing any fishing, so we didn't have fishing poles. We had some reddish rubber patches used to repair kayaks, which we strung on some wire and put bread crumbs on it. We then threw it in the water and within thirty seconds after we threw it in the water, bang! The bait was hit by a three-foot long fish. Every time we casted the makeshift line, about thirty to forty-five seconds later we would catch a big fish. We decided no one was to catch fish unless we were within three feet from a good landing place. There is no use in dragging excess fish.

Jumped From Ledge to Ledge

I was in the back of the lead kayak, and we were paddling along. The whole time there was a noise in the trees that sounded like a breeze and it was getting progressively stronger. Then the two of us realized it was the sound of a waterfall. We came around a corner, and saw that the stream disappeared about 120 yards ahead! We shouted to the other canoes and we paddled as fast as we could, but all we could do was paddle back but all the boat did was stand still. So we turned the boat sideways and back paddled the kayak. The kayak drifted towards the shore and equally fast towards the forty foot waterfall.

We reached the shore with me in the back of the kayak holding onto a rock on the shore and my companion hanging over one foot of the canyon. The others were trying to get to us as fast as possible. There was dense brush and about ten yards to go until they would have reached us. My partner was still over the canyon and I was in the back of the kayak holding onto a rock on the shore. Although it was a sturdy hold, I was getting tired as the back of the kayak was starting to rise as front was sinking. The rest of the group arrived just when I had to let go and. They went running to get hold of the kayak. As the back of the kayak was rising over the waterfall canyon, they grabbed it and pulled the entire kayak back to the top of the canyon. If the others came four seconds later, we would have gone over the cliff to our death. It was the Canadian government's fault because they never gave us a map showing that there was a waterfall or saying that there might be one. We would have been extra careful if we knew there was a waterfall and we would have been back earlier.

However, we were still faced with the problem of the cliff because the trail we needed to follow was at its bottom. In order to get down, we had to get down from one ledge to another. The cliff was about forty feet deep. There were small, little flat ledges about a foot to a foot and a half wide and about four to six feet long with three to six feet between each ledge, leading down to the bottom. I led going down and with the kayak on my shoulder, I jumped from ledge to ledge, and only looked as far down as the next ledge. When I reached the bottom, I looked above and saw one person in the group had a camera and took pictures of me going down that cliff. Some months later we met at his home to see the pictures that were taken. When I saw the pictures of all of us descending that cliff on those little jumps I began to appreciate how far down it was. I was sick to my stomach. The funny thing is I did not feel sick when I was actually going down the cliff. If I had looked down at the bottom while I was descending, I would have been scared. All I thought was to look to the next ledge. I could not look around; five others had to do the same thing. The bottom was at the end of a ravine perpendicular to the river. Up at the other side of this ravine there was a three foot wide path which animals had been using to get up to the continuation of the shore of the river beyond the waterfall. We walked two hundred yards further beyond the path to where we were able to use our kayaks and we put them back into the water.

Black Bears Love Blueberries

Further down the river there was a small but very interesting island a half mile long with trees and plants scattered on it. We continued on another mile and it finally looked like we had a slow and wide river close to a lake. We prepared to arrive at the dam the next day. The place where we landed was at the edge of a two to three mile area of blueberries that were completely ripe and ready to be harvested. Six foot pine trees mixed within the blueberry plants. Another scout and I decided to go collect the berries with a ten gallon pail. We collected the blueberries by pulling the 10-gallon pail along the ground by its handle and letting the blueberries drop in the pail. We ate some of the blueberries as we went back to our camp. We were eating some of the blueberries we collected when my partner said, "Is that a bear following us?" It was getting to be night and since black bears love blueberries, just hearing that scared the heck out of me. I jumped and looked around, but there weren't any bears. Luckily there were just small trees, four to six feet high, covering an area of about a mile or two. The smaller trees had probably been the result of a fire a long time before. Back at the camp, we cleaned out the pail and prepared a crust with some flour to put it in the bottom of the pail that we collected the blueberries with. Then we added a little sugar despite the berries being delicious. We had a six inch high pile of berries. In addition, we had fish and other things to eat for supper. The next day we had a good breakfast and prepared the food that we would be eating in the middle of the lake, where land would be out of sight. We were using a compass as our guide. We had to paddle all day long to get to the dam. We prepared lunch before we left the shore and half way there we rested and ate. At that time there was still no sign of the shore, but we knew the direction since we were using the compass. Eventually, we reached the dam and our parents were waiting to pick us up. Our Boy Scout trip ended there, at Big Beaver Dam in early June.

Escanaba

At the end of the Boy Scout trip my father picked me up at the dam and drove us back through Sault St. Marie. We drove 340 miles to Escanaba, Michigan. My father dropped me off at a hotel in Escanaba, where I knew no one. He continued on the five hundred miles to home by himself. With ten dollars in my pocket, I had to take care of myself until school started on September 10th. There was a hotel with accommodations for minors that would provide a place to sleep in exchange for working around the place. Jobs included cleaning rooms, picking vegetables and so on. I picked cucumbers with another fellow. The smaller cucumbers were unmarketable, so we took them for ourselves. After three days, we had a full barrel of the small cucumbers, about two and a half feet high and a foot and half wide. We added water, got some dill from the roadside, added some salt and let it mature. After two days we ate the whole barrel of pickles. I had never had pickles like that before; they had just the right amount of dill and salt!

Trespassing

After a while I grew tired of picking vegetables and decided I'd like to do something else. I hitch hiked fifty miles west, away from Escanaba to where there was a farmhouse that looked like it could use some help. They did indeed need some extra hands. I learned how to hitch up a team of horses and make the two horses work together. I got a little bored after doing that for a while too, so I caught a freight train going west. The train stopped at Rice Lake, Wisconsin. I mistakenly failed to recognize that Rice Lake was a division point. At such locations, they rearranged the railroad cars in order to be dropped off one at a time as they went along the track. All division points have a guard day and night, unlike at other train stops. At Rice Lake, they found me sleeping in an empty box car. They went and told the police, who came and picked me up, put me in jail and charged me with trespassing on railroad property. So I spent the night in jail. In the morning they fed me, took me out to the edge of town and told me to never come back again. I never did! (Years later when I mentioned Rice Lake to the librarian at Princeton University, he said "I know Rice Lake; I was born and raised twenty miles north of there. I don't blame you for not going back!") Some day I might go back to see what Rice Lake is like now.

Riding the Rails Along the Way

From there I went to Minneapolis, where there was a big rail yard. There were seven or eight bums who traveled around together and shared their earnings. Two of us would go into town to buy canned food to bring back to the group. We'd gather bits of wood for a small fire and eat. At around noon, we'd spot an authority figure and move on to another spot to avoid being bugged or bothered. I'd live like that for awhile, traveling with different groups of bums. I continued riding the freight trains with this group of bums up towards the Dakotas. While in Minneapolis, I looked for a train that would head towards South Dakota. There probably would be a lot of wheat out there that needed to be harvested, so I figured I could help out. I jumped on the freight train towards South Dakota to get a job, and fifteen minutes later in a small town in South Dakota, I obtained a job with a crew harvesting wheat. The harvesting team cut the dry wheat with its tablets, collected the wheat tablets and let the straw accumulate into large piles that I would also sleep and live in. I got up for work when the sun rose and noon time was when the farmer fed the team. Occasionally there was a farmer's house on the land we worked on. They gave us as much food as we could eat. At night time I went to sleep in my pile of straw. That's the way I lived for about two months. For those two months, it never rained. The crew went through South Dakota and continued on to North Dakota. In those days you could register to get a square mile of land and if after three years you had done something to improve the quality of that square mile, the land would be yours to keep. Everybody there owned land in terms of square miles. When it came time to harvest wheat, one would continue one mile up then one mile down until the farm was clear of that farmer's wheat.

To ride large commercial waterproof rail cars, one would have to know where the detectives who were removing bums like me were positioned on the trains. One would have to outwit the yard detective by anticipating where the detective was going and where he would be hiding. One had to know which end of the train the detective would start from. It ended up that he went pretty far up ahead, out of sight, so we crossed over the railroad tracks at that time. The problem was that by the time the detective would be halfway down the train, the train would already be going fifteen miles an hour, therefore everybody who rode the freight trains had to know how to go for the front of any car! There were well-to-do people up in places like Scarsdale, where the executives from New York City lived, going to places like Manhattan by railroad and they would some-times run after a railroad car that had already started to move in the direction of the city. These people would always go for the rear opening of a car! This could result in them falling between the railroad cars and losing a leg. However if they went for the front of a car they would only risk falling off on their side and just get bruised. The well-to-do people who went for the rears of the railroad cars were naïve. Any good bum would tell you to always go for the front of a railroad car!

One day I was traveling with a bum from central North Dakota to a place in the north where cattle were raised. The bum said that he was an "electrician". When we got off the train there were a lot of cattle in the area and there was also a large one floor building with no windows but a lot of water faucets located around it. However, these faucets did not work. I thought if we were able to get inside we might be able to get cleaned up, but it was locked so he took his electrician's tools and within forty-five seconds he had the door unlocked. He was actually a professional thief! We then went in, showered, cleaned up after ourselves and then locked the door on our way out. He went on his way and I went on mine. I had to catch the next train to see my grand-parents.

I caught a freight train to Minot, North Dakota and hopped off to visit my grandpar-ents. The next morning they took me to the railroad yard to catch the train to Chicago. On my last 700 mile non-stop train ride from Minot to Chicago, I rode an express train with one hundred and twenty cars full of wheat and two engineers at the front of the train. The engineers had a cot to sleep in so they could take turns sleeping and driving. The train was moving about fifty to sixty miles an hour and since it was an express with a big load, the train would not be slowing down or making any stops. It would take too much time to slow down and get going again. Every car was loaded to the top with wheat. I was riding on the top of one of the cars and I was getting very drowsy. I rolled down one side of the car and my legs were hanging over the side of the car while I dozed off. When I woke up I grabbed the top and proceeded to climb back up. I never fell asleep on the train again, despite being on top of that train for a whole fifty-three hours. The train did not slow down until we pulled into the train yard in Chicago where the large silos collected the wheat. I slipped off and caught the bus to my home in Oak Park.

I Got Home

I got home on a Saturday afternoon and went promptly to bed. I slept all through the rest of that Saturday and all through the following Sunday. On Monday morning I hurried to get dressed and go to school. It was the first day of the school program. My parents never heard about what happened until I got home from school that day.

When my father left me in Escanaba, I only had ten dollars in my pocket. When I arrived back home, two hundred dollars were in my pocket. That was an incredible amount of money at that time since the country was in the Great Depression. I was quite confident after my experience with the railroad cars that I could support myself. I could go to the University of Illinois without any help from my father.

I felt an enormous amount of freedom. My father couldn't make me do anything I didn't want to do. If he said, "You have to…" I could have said, "I'll catch a freight train!" He knew that I knew how to ride the freight trains and do quite well for myself, so he had to back down. He could only get me to do something if I was willing to do it. He had no way of putting any pressure on me, and it infuriated him.

Seven and a Half Steps

One day, a month before the end of my senior year in high school, I was late going to the school swimming pool. I rushed down the steps and down I went! I fell down seven and half steps! My tibia, the bone between the knee and the ankle, popped out of my skin and went back into the ankle. The bone carried the bacteria on the surface of the skin into the ankle joint and thus caused an infection in my left leg. In the hospital, they had me in all kinds of supports for my leg and the pain was just terrible because they never gave me enough pain medicine to relieve the pain. I was left in agony the whole time. They considered amputating the foot and ankle. Fortunately sulfa drugs had just recently been invented so they decided to try the new medicine first. I felt like jumping out of the hospital window. Lo and behold, twenty-four hours later my ankle began to heal. The tibia healed and went back as close as it could to its normal position, although it angled off about 15°. That is the position it has been in *ever* since.

From then on, I'd bandage my left leg day in and day out. If I didn't bandage it correctly, the skin would ulcerate and take a month to six weeks to heal so it was crucial to keep pressure on the leg. Some twenty to thirty years later, I noticed some swelling in my right leg and began bandaging that as well. I bandaged both legs for about forty years.

On the left leg, which had been fused together, a really dense white area where the infection was showed up on the x-ray. This was a sign that it still persisted. As the years have gone by, it has totally disappeared. Some twelve or fifteen years later, I stubbed my toe and had another x-ray. That's when I found out that the infection was completely gone. I showed the x-rays to another doctor and by then, there was no trace that there had ever been an ankle joint in my left leg. Thirty years later it began to hurt again and I had another x-ray of my left ankle and showed the x-ray to another doctor. There was a smooth even bone going past the place where it should be an ankle. The doctor said "Oh my gosh! There is no ankle, what happened?" and I replied "There is no motion in that ankle". The doctor than exclaimed "There is no ankle!"

Student at Princeton University

When it came time to go to college, my father said, "I don't give a damn where you go, as long as it is at least 1,000 miles from home." I got accepted to Princeton and Harvard and decided to go to Princeton. I looked it up on a map and it was only 980 miles away. I went to father and said, "Dad, I'd like to go to Princeton, but it's only 980 miles from our house. Do you mind if I'm so close?" He forgave the last twenty miles and I went to Princeton University.

Having Breakfast in Bed

It had been a tradition at Princeton University for the freshmen to try to steal the bell clapper on top of Nassau Hall. Nassau Hall is a 4 floored building in the front of Princeton University that is 20 yards high. If the clapper didn't ring one day then you didn't have to go to class! Since I knew I would have to climb a drain pipe to get to the bell, I began to practice rope climbing. I broke the University's record for rope climbing, which was fifty feet in 7.6 seconds. I was strong enough to get to the clapper, but when I got to the gutter at the top of the drain pipe around Nassau Hall, my hands were too cold and I could hardly hold on anymore. I was right at the edge of the building and the vines around the pipes were not strong enough to support me. The pipe was too big to slide down, so I had no choice but to jump, and down I went.

My body landed flat on the ground with my face up, feet bent down, and knees only slightly bent. When I hit the ground, my spine was vertically straight. I suffered a perfect compression fracture of two vertebrae. After I hit the ground, the first thing I did was wiggle my toes. I was able to wiggle all my toes so I knew my spine hadn't been seriously hurt, but I had a serious backache. Vertebrate spines L-1 and L-2 were crushed smoothly and evenly (I ended up losing two inches in height because of this) and I told a colleague that I wouldn't move until he got a doctor there! They got a university doctor to come out and they put me on a stretcher to the infirmary. Before this escapade, I had written an unfinished letter to my mother. While I was in the infirmary, I finished the letter. I ended it by writing, "Having breakfast in bed – John."

That's Our Son

My parents heard about the incident on the radio. "A boy from Oak Park, Illinois…" (I was the only boy from Oak Park, Illinois that attended Princeton University). My father took the train to Princeton to see what happened. He wanted to bring me back to Chicago because in Princeton the doctors treated injuries like that with six months in a plaster cast. In Chicago and the rest of the west they used a plaster cast that would put you back on your feet in ten days, so my father took me to Chicago by train. They had to take a window out of the train to be able to fit me on the train with my stretcher. Back in Chicago, they took the window out again, took me out, replaced the window and took me to the hospital. They put me in a plaster cast that was an inch and a half thick and lined with cloth on the inside. It went from my groin up to my armpits, solid around my entire body. There was a four inch by six inch rectangular hole in the area of the stomach to allow for expansion when eating. If the hole was filled, I had to stop eating. Even a half glass of water could have caused me to vomit! As soon as there was more space at the opening I could eat or drink again.

Tough as Nails

The day before I went back to Princeton, I attended a dance with a girl I had dated that year. She was in the class behind me during high school. We were out there waltzing around with my suit concealing my cast. When we were swinging around, one fellow bumped into me, smashing his elbow. He went off the floor rubbing his elbow and he exclaimed, "Boy, there's someone out there tough as nails!" He didn't know who it was, but it was a really tough kid! My partner kept her distance from me and did not get injured.

The first day back at Princeton was a Monday morning. I had a freshman English class. I put two chairs back to back about four feet apart and lay down across them, with my hands behind my head. The plaster cast supported me easily. When the instructor arrived, I said "I'm just resting!" He was puzzled and shook his head, not knowing what to do or say.

Even after all that, I finally did steal the clapper which caught the attention of the *New York Times*. They printed a front page story with a photograph stating, "he will be productive, if he lives that long." There was also an article published in a column of *Time* magazine titled, "Boys Will Be Boys".

Boys Will Be Boys
TIME Magazine - Monday, May 06, 1940

Stealing the bell clapper from the tower of old Nassau Hall is so persistent a custom at Princeton that the university does a profitable business: the university keeps a barrel of spare clappers in reserve and fines students $30 a steal. One dark night two months later a freshman, John C. Seed, 19, of Oak Park, IL, eluded the bored watchman and shimmied up a drain pipe. He got to the top and was holding onto the gutter, he lost his hold, falling thirty-five feet to the ground. Freshman Seed went to a Chicago hospital, where his father was a physician. He had two damaged vertebrae and no sign of any breakage.

Like the boy in a cartoon by British cartoonist Henry Bateman, who went to prison for breathing hard on a glass case in the British Museum and returned, a decrepit old man, to breathe his defiant, dying breath on the same forbidden glass; John Seed did not give up his high resolve. On the last fortnight he returned to college, strapped in a plaster cast from waist to shoulders. He spurned the university's offer to end the contest by giving him a clapper.

One stormy night last week, John Seed, still strapped in his cast, tried again. This time he went in by a door, climbed a ladder to the belfry and there pried open a locked door with a four-foot crowbar. With two companions he tugged at the clapper for half an hour, at length pulling it loose! Next day he proudly confessed his theft! Crushed, the university waived its $30 fine.

OAK PARK YOUTH AT PRINCETON IS INJURED IN PRANK

Princeton, N. J., March 10 [Special].—John C. Seed, 18 years old, of 923 North Elmwood street, Oak Park, Ill., suffered severe back injuries late last night when he fell 35 feet to the ground while attempting to steal the clapper from the bell of Nassau hall—a feat that has been a traditional challenge to Princeton freshmen for generations.

John C. Seed.

Two other freshmen who were standing watch below called an ambulance to remove the injured boy to the university infirmary.

The tradition of stealing the clapper is so old that its origin has been lost in antiquity, but many prominent Princeton graduates still cherish stolen clappers as mementos of their youth.

Seed is the son of Dr. Lindon Seed, a Chicago surgeon. He prepared at Oak Park High school for Princeton.

THE OAK PARKE

John Seed Hurt in Freshman Prank At Princeton

John C. Seed, son of Dr. and Mrs. Lindon Seed, 923 Elmwood avenue, and a freshman at Princeton university, fell thirty-five feet from the belfry of Nassau Hall on the campus Saturday night. Two vertebrae were broken, and the young man was severely stunned, but will recover from the injuries.

John was attempting to perform a feat that has baffled Princeton freshmen for generations; stealing the clapper from the bell on Nassau hall. The young man's father, Dr. Seed, who is a practicing physician in Chicago, received word Sunday of his son's injuries, and left for Princeton by plane at once. He phoned to Mrs. Seed Sunday night that John will recover from the injuries.

John graduated last June from Oak Park and River Forest high school.

Climbs, Falls, Climbs Again! Gets His Bell

"Home of the Brave," village of the bell-tower climbers, that's Oak Park. John C. Seed, son of Dr. and Mrs. Lindon Seed of 923 North Elmwood, has contributed his bit to make it so.

John, who is a Princeton freshman, made a promise a few months ago that he meant to keep. "The bell clapper in Nassau hall must come down," he said, "and I think I'm the man to do it." So up climbed John to where the bell did hang, and down he came again with an awful bang. Net result: two broken vertebrae and . . . no clapper.

For one month he lay in the infirmary and thought things over in a plaster cast, but it took sterner stuff than a little medical cement and water to stop him.

At the first opportunity he was back at the tower cast and all figuring out the odds like Moe Annenberg never did. There'd be lots of ground and lot of distance beneath him and maybe a little Seed too, if he slipped; a stone wall in front of him and sadly enough, not much of anything in back of him.

University officials offered him a clapper. Seed said, "no."

Last week the Nassau bell failed to do its usual stuff. It looked like Seed had the bell in the bag.

Superintendent of Princeton Buildings, Edward A. MacMillan, who is curious like you and me, stated that the usual $30 and costs would be waived if the guilty lad would fess up.

Out of the night that darkened them stepped John who said, "I did it, with two little freshies to help me."

John is now a happy boy. He has his cherished bell banger and is sure that "honesty is the best policy," whereas Washington still has his doubts. His old man licked him, if you remember the story.

CH 11, 1940

Princeton Frosh Hurt Trying To Get To Bell

JOHN C. SEED

PRINCETON, N. J.—Seed, member of the freshman class, received serious back injuries yesterday when he fell while making a traditional attempt to get the clapper of the bell atop of Nassau Hall.

Princeton Freshman Seriously Hurt in Fall Trying to Steal Nassau Hall Bell Clapper

Special to THE NEW YORK TIMES.

PRINCETON, N. J., March 10—Falling thirty-five feet to the ground while engaged in an unsuccessful attempt to steal the clapper from the bell of Nassau Hall—a feat that has been a traditional challenge to Princeton freshmen for generations—John C. Seed, 18 years old, of Oak Park, Ill., fractured two vertebrae late last night.

Seed was attempting to scale the wall of the Continental Congress room at the rear of Nassau Hall, with the aid of a water spout at one corner of the building and the ivy that mantles the walls of the ancient structure, when he either lost his grasp or the ivy gave way. He fell to a boardwalk below.

Two other freshmen were standing watch below to warn him if proctors should approach. They saw him fall and realized he was badly hurt. The two youths, Richard A. Hord of Lexington, Ky., and Raymond A. Bieksha of Arlington, N. J., called the proctors, who summoned Dr. David M. Keedy, resident physician at the Princeton University Infirmary.

Dr. Keedy had an ambulance brought to the scene to remove the injured boy to the infirmary, where he was resting comfortably today. Dr. Wilbur H. York, chairman of the Department of Health and Physical Education of the university, said Seed fractured his first and second lumbar vertebrae.

Seed is the son of Dr. Lindon Seed, a prominent Chicago surgeon. He prepared at Oak Park High for Princeton. It is expected that after a stay of about ten days in the infirmary here he will be removed to his home for convalescence.

The tradition of stealing the clapper from the Nassau Hall bell is so old that its origin has been lost in antiquity, but many prominent Princeton graduates still cherish stolen clappers as mementos of their youth. Because it is attempted repeatedly every year by daring freshmen, the university imposes a fine of $30 on those caught with stolen clappers, but there is no other disciplinary action.

Oak Park youth keeps pledge to 'steal' bell

John C. Seed, Princeton freshman from Oak Park, kept his self-styled "perverse" promise to steal the bell clapper from the belfry of Nassau hall, friends learned here today.

Seed broke two vertebrae March 9 when he fell in an attempt at the traditional freshman stunt. A month later he returned to classes—his torso in a plaster cast. Spurning an offer of university officials to give him a clapper, Seed announced he'd try again. The plaster cast won't be removed for another two months.

Nassau's bell stopped striking early Sunday. Two alumni told an official they had taken it and were forgiven. Rumor persisted on the campus Seed was the actual "culprit." Supt. of Buildings Edward A. MacMillan announced if Seed confessed the usual undergraduate fee of $30 would be waived.

Seed finally admitted he and two other students had taken the clapper after four hours' work.

My Family

44

My Religious Development

When my parents and family moved to Oak Park, Illinois, they sent me off to Christian Churches every Sunday to get me out of the house in the mornings. During our first couple of years there they would take me to different churches and then would pick me up when the services were over. After two years, I began walking and biking to and from church. I went to a variety of churches, but never saw or heard of my parents ever going to church.

During my last two years in high school, a friend of mine was going to the Pilgrim Congregational Church, so I went with him. One day, the minister announced that there was going to be a series of twelve talks about the beliefs of the church after the regular sermon. Fourteen children, including myself, attended and at the end of the series, the minister, Mr. Coe, asked for a show of hands of those who wanted to join the church. Thirteen hands went up, excluding me. He then asked for a show of hands of those who did not want to join and my hand was the only hand up. The minister asked, "Why not?" and I said, "Because the Presbyterians say 'this', the Lutherans say 'that', the Episcopalians teach 'the other", and I just don't know who is right. I don't want to join the wrong church!" As I started to go on talking, he stopped me and said, "Stop, I will talk to you later." We never talked, but twenty-nine or thirty years later he became the leader of the Pilgrim Congregational Churches.

My best friend in high school was a Christian Scientist like his parents. His father was a colonel in the United States Army and an engineer in charge of dams as well as dam locks in the Ohio, Indiana, Illinois and Mississippi River. One summer he had me and his son join him, bringing our girlfriends along, as he went down the rivers on a boat inspecting docks, dams, locks and the conditions of the depths of the stream as well as the conditions of the shores. We slept and ate on board the boat and it was great fun.

In the first year at Princeton, all students were required to attend a religious service Sunday mornings at the large church on Washington Street. Whenever we went, we had to sign in a book, to prove that we were there. Princeton University had a magnificent church to the left of their central university building and had a Christian Presbyterian service there every Sunday morning. If students went to other Christian services, like the Saint Paul's Catholic Church, then they had to sign a booklet at that church like the rest of us. The students usually attended the services at the Presbyterian chapel at the university. Princeton University started as a part of the Presbyterian Church many years before 1900. In 1939 the church still had an influence on the university, but the church lost its influence after World War II. The Presbyterian Church remained active in Princeton.

In 1980 the priest at St. Paul's Catholic Church started to have services at 5:00 p.m. on Sundays in addition to the masses in the mornings. Father DeMarcellis was the lecturer, a task that a layman usually does, which involves reading two passages from the bible that are not from the gospel, since the gospel is read by a priest. After mass I came up to father DeMarcellis and volunteered to be a lecturer. At the church I attended in Scarsdale I was a lecturer. Later on in mass, when it was time to receive communion, Father DeMarcellis gave me communion and asked me to give out communion to the rest of the congregation. He then said "You're a Eucharistic minister" and so I was made a lecturer and Eucharistic minister. In 2004, I had some trouble climbing up to the altar so I was unable to continue to serve as a Eucharistic Minister at St. Paul's Catholic Church. I still attended mass and was seated on the first row near the aisle, at the right side if you were facing the priest.

Princeton Institute for the Science & Technology of Materials

One of the first computers invented was located at the Princeton Institute for the Science and Technology of Materials and was designed by John Von Neumann. Shortly after his death, my friend Forman Acton and another man, Bigellio took over the work with the computer. These early computers used vacuum tubes for logic circuits in much the same way that modern computers use semiconductors.. Bigellio, who was an electrician, was the man responsible for maintaining the computer. He was also a big player of chimes, producing a sound that is very unusual. He was a bell ringer.

The computer equipment was so large it took up three rooms. This instrument was a bit quirky. It would work only when it rained. We were using the computers to do various things. I developed a calculation and a system to record the morphine I used on my patients. I was seeing patients in New York City and came down to Princeton three or four afternoons or evenings to use the machines, if it was not raining. I always called Forman before I came down to Princeton to see if it was raining or if it was likely to rain. Forman and I began making more complicated programs, like addition and subtraction, which were very difficult to put together. At the beginning we would punch in "1010101010", off and on. The big step was at the end of 1950 when IBM came out with a program. This was the beginning of modern computers. They were all put together in packages and were very well designed. Companies continued to make improvements on computers and still computers today are constantly improving.

In 1960, the Department of Physics at Princeton started to buy computers. Eight to ten students would be running the programs. Three or four of us would check the common machine programs to see if there were problems and then we would fix them. One of the problems that came up frequently was the printer. The printer would sometimes cease to work because of electronic activity in the air, which is called "static". The next thing the electrons in the environment needed was electronic grounding out of the system. I knew how the computers worked and one evening I put a humidifier inside the computer. When the computer was not working I would pour water into the humidifier that was inside the computer and the computer would work. The computer just needed the right amount of moisture. That was my contribution to the development of computers. Thirteen years later they moved the computers to another room. In doing this they found out that the wire that went to the electric grounding did not go to the ground. This caused the mild electrical activity that was always in the air to cause problems. They made sure they grounded the computers properly in this new room and when they did this; they no longer needed a humidifier.

Pre-Computers

Around that time, I spent two to three weeks putting together an equation while I was lying down on my back in the library trying to think. Finally I got the equation together and worked it well. After I had the equation, I started working with a desk calculator and I spent fifty hours doing the first twelve minutes of the test run. I thought there might be a thing like computers that could solve my equations much more quickly. There was a big computer at Harvard, but they were not doing much with it.

Van Neumann Computers

In 1956, I called a good friend of mine and asked him what a computer can do and how someone could get access to one. It turns out that my friend James Arnold was in charge of the Van Neumann computer, one of the world's first computers, and that's the one I learned to program on, forty numbers at a time, pushing them on and off. It started and then all of a sudden, there wasn't any warning that it was not working. I loaded it in again and proved that it would run very nicely. Fifty-five hours doing calculations by hand was to be done by having the computer do it in about one minute.

If It Is Raining the Computer Works

When I started teaching computer applications in medicine, there were four people credited with being able to improve the machine when it failed or did not work properly; and I was one of those four. If it was raining outside the computers would work but on hot sunny and dry days they would not work. One problem we ran into often was that the printer would not print properly. I mostly had to help people who said that the printer seemed to be acting as if it had static problems because of a lack of humidity. They did not understand that it was that the computer was not grounded for the electron. Despite their opinion, I obtained a humidifier and put it inside the printer and put water into it and the humidity in the air solved the static problems. I always had an unusual water carrier. I would lift up the piece of metal covering the printer and put my hand down with this strange thing and poured the water. Fifteen minutes later the printer worked again because the problem was indeed static. The lack of moisture in the air allowed static activity to occur. I recognized that was the problem with the printer and nobody else would believe it. It turned out some ten years later, they moved the printer and they checked all the other machines and none of those machines were grounded electrically with a wire. All of the machines had the wires to get to the ground, but the final wire never got to the ground. That's why there was static activity in the printers. They did not find out until twenty years later why pouring water into the computer enabled it to work. I was proud when they tore up the third floor of the Union News Schools (the electrical engineering part) and found their mistake. All the equipment was inspected, collected and grounded to one piece of ground, but the one piece of equipment that was supposed to be grounded was not. We needed some moisture in the air. I found a spot to pour in water and if someone was having trouble, I would just go over and add some water. The air has electrons. Electrical charges accumulate in the machine, so it had to get grounded. When there is moisture in the air the electrostatics will dissipate.

The Atom Bomb

My first course in Princeton University was Organic Chemistry and during the laboratory experiments my partner was Forman Acton, who has remained my friend ever since. Forman was always annoyed with me because when we were doing experiments, I always wanted to do each of them over again to be sure we got the same results. I developed a group of eight friends during my first semester. We remained friends during our entire time at Princeton. The only other name I remember from those days was James Arnold.

During my freshman year at Princeton in September of 1939, it was discovered that firing neutrons at uranium 235 generated large amounts of heat and the uranium 235 changed into powder. When our group heard of it, we all thought of what a good bomb it would be, if only someone could only get enough uranium 235. We discussed how someone could make the uranium 235 into a bomb and how that person could set it off. However, there wasn't much interest because one would not be able to get enough of the uranium 235.

Toward the end of my first year at Princeton, it was clear that the U.S. was getting involved with the war. There was pressure put on the universities to accelerate our learning. Classes covered more material than usual. There were more examinations per week. No holidays, the stress continued throughout the year. For me, graduation was at the end of June after three years. I never turned in my thesis, but still was able to go to Harvard Medical School, which was quite an honor. The war was still on, but fortunately they were not drafting medical students.

Forman Acton stayed at Princeton University continuing on to The Graduate School of Chemical Engineering. After about one year he was drafted for military service. There were eight of us in that same class who kept together and Forman was the only one of us that was drafted. My other friend James Arnold went to the University of Chicago to get his PhD. While he was there, he told his supervisor about the possibility of finding the age of ancient wood by measuring how much carbon fourteen had disappeared. Arnold stayed at Chicago for a while and then disappeared into the atom bomb project. Other members of the group also went off to academic affairs and then, disappeared into programs related to atom bombs. However no one went into the army, expect Forman Acton.

Acton came to see me in medical school to tell me that the army was planning to make an atomic bomb. The reason he thought so was that he noted that Einstein, Oppenheimer, Bohr, Wigner, Szilard, and Fermi were all meeting frequently and in small, random groups. All of these men were experts in psychoanalysis, mathematics and nuclear physics. I told Acton that is was impossible to get the amount of uranium 235 that was needed to make an atomic bomb. I said they are intelligent professors, who can help make anything. One thing the country needed was better rockets. Acton could not be influenced. Shortly after that, Acton was drafted. After that, he never talked about atomic bombs to any one else but me. After being in the military for awhile, he gave a paper to his lieutenant that said, "I would like to be assigned to the atomic bomb project", and was signed "Private Acton".

Forman Acton and John Seed

About ten days later an order came from General Leslie R. Groves in Washington, DC that Forman was to be put in prison and nobody was to talk to him. Around that time Forman's mother, who lived in Salem, NJ, (his hometown) observed that there were a whole lot of men in their twenties and thirties in grocery stores and other ordinary places for about two days. No one in town knew who these men were or where they came from. A few days later, Forman was sent to Camp Croft in South Carolina, which was just fifteen miles below North Carolina, for more basic training: marching, saluting, rifle shooting etc. While training he earned the rank of private and learned to march and fire guns on hot dusty days.

Six weeks later, Forman began feeling that he might better employ his technical training. He wrote to the Tennessee Eastman Corporation. A little over a month later, Major Russell came to the military at Camp Croft and asked for Forman. Along with some other Croft trainees, they were quietly rounded up, told to pack up and were shipped by night train to Ohio State University in Columbus, Ohio. They were housed under the football stadium, but given no duties and told nothing. Each one of them in the group had an interview with Major Russell. After all the interviews were completed, about thirty of them were told to pack and report to the Columbus train station at 5:00 pm.

A six hour train ride got them to Knoxville, Tennessee which was the first time they knew where they were going. They were bused to an Army barracks area, given bedding and told to sleep until 9 in the morning. Then Forman was instructed to take the local bus to Y-12 and report to Colonel Ruhoff. The bus driver took him to Y-12 and a guard at the chemical plant gate took him to Colonel Ruhoff. Next to Colonel Ruhoff sat Major Russell. The huge plant was separating U-235 from U-238 in mass spectroscopes, using magnets with cores about twelve feet in diameter. They really were doing this atom-by-atom to achieve only very small, low yields with lots of magnets. The plant was built and operated by Tennessee Eastman Corporation under contract with the Army Corps of Engineers. It was basically run by Lt. Col. John Ruhoff.

Uranium Bombs Were Being Made

Forman joined Ruhoff's staff of about twenty engineers who kept track of operations. He was free to go anywhere in the plant and all his questions, as well as the other staff members, were fully answered. Only in one matter was Forman unique, only HE kept the records of the total amount of Uranium suitable for bombs that had been obtained from this process. This was the only piece of information that was officially considered to be a Top Secret.

After a few weeks Forman applied for the week's leave that was due to all soldiers who finished their basic training. He visited his hometown of Salem, NJ and went to Princeton University to see the remaining classmates. It was Sunday when he arrived in Princeton, so Forman and three friends had a nice lunch at the Peacock Inn, four houses north of

Stockton Street in Princeton. They then went to the social building at the university, which was empty at the time, to play a few hands of bridge.

After a while one of the friends, named Eliot Woodridge, noticed a stranger in a communicating room and asked the other bridge players if they knew who that might be. They did not know, but they asked Eliot why he was curious. "Because he was also sitting at an adjacent table from us at lunch," said Eliot.

Alarm bells were ringing in Forman's mind. He was going to New York City for dinner at a friend's house. He was neither surprised, nor pleased, to find the stranger boarding the same five o'clock train. He clearly was being tailed, but by whom? Was he friend or foe? Forman ditched the guy in the Grand Central Subway Station in New York (There is no better place to lose somebody than in Grand Central Station, with the massive numbers of subway riders) and completed his weekend without seeing the stranger again. Several months later, after Forman had officially met one of Oak Ridge's intelligence operators, he asked him if the stranger was working for us or the Russians and the stranger was in fact one of us. He was sent to follow Forman because of Forman's special knowledge about total production of Y-12.

Forman was allowed out of Oak Ridge one time, but guards were sent with him. If he went swimming there was always someone watching him. One day in the first week of May, Oppenheimer, the man in charge of making the atomic bomb, sent a letter to the General in charge at Oak Ridge asking when "X" amount of U-235 would be available. Wigner, a professor at Princeton University on Oppenheimer staff, suggested to Oppenheimer that he should also send a letter to his friend, Corporal Acton suggesting that he might know. While the General gave a date of some time in the middle of August, Forman said it would be ready on May 9th at eleven o'clock in the morning.

The First Atom Bomb is Done

On May 9th at 9 in the morning, a plane from Alamo arrived. The pilot asked for the uranium needed to make the atomic bomb. Forman said, "It is not ready, I said at eleven o'clock." At that time, he produced it. From then on the letters were to Corporal Acton, with a copy to the commanding general. After that, there was a test of the atom bomb. Then 3 days later they again obtained enough U-235 and dropped an atomic bomb on Hiroshima, which caused vast numbers of deaths and caused destruction of buildings in Northern Japan. On the day after Hiroshima, I received an anonymous postcard that on the back said, "I told you so". I turned the card over and there was my name and address; up in the corner was a stamp from Oak Ridge, TN.

About a month later, our group happened to be around the Chicago area at the same time. James Arnold was working at the University of Chicago and lived nearby. I was living with my parents in Oak Park waiting for the order to go to the Army Chemical

Warfare center. I had finished my training in army medical operations during warfare. Arnold and I were having supper together on Thursday evenings in downtown Chicago. One day we got together in Washington Park, sitting a hundred yards from where anyone who could hear us, as we discussed the details necessary to make atom bombs and fire them. Everyone, except me, had something to do with the making of the atom bomb. Thank goodness at that time, the government didn't know of the discussion we had at that dinner.

I Went to Medical School

During my second year at Princeton, World War II began. Vacations along with all the major physics professors disappeared. The biology courses that I needed to get into medical school were taught in the summer. I enjoyed them and did well, but really liked physics more. I began to worry if I really wanted to be a doctor. My father was chairman of the surgical department at the University of Illinois and I knew about the kind of people that he associated with, but I knew a lot about physics as well.

That fall, I took a course on atomic spectra that was taught by a graduate student in Physics. In the first course, he was not covering anything that I had not already known. I came back during the middle of the semester and he still was not teaching anything that was new to me. I did not come to any more lectures. At the end of the course he called me to see if I was still enrolled. I said "yes". He told me I was the only one in the course that was not a physics major. The physics majors had to take an exam covering several courses in physics and not any exams on individual courses. The "teacher" made up an examination for me to take. I passed it without any errors.

I was not about to ask the graduate student about a career in physics. With no advice, I chickened out and decided to go into medicine. I applied for Columbia and Harvard. I was interviewed at both and I was impressed by the doctor from Columbia and not from the one from Harvard. I was asked why I wanted to be a doctor, and my answer was, "I have always wanted to be a doctor. When other five and six year old boys wanted to be policemen or firemen, I wanted to be a doctor, and I am going to be a doctor." My friends were aghast that I could be so adamant. I figured out how to be so confident without any difficulty. Being in the top 1% of the students in my class at Princeton University and having a well known father who was a surgeon was enough to boost my self-esteem. Anyhow, I was accepted to both medical schools. I sent a telegram to my father telling him that I had been accepted to both and I was going to Columbia. Three hours later, I received a telegram from him, which read, "If you do, you can pay for your own way for the rest of your education." So I decided to matriculate to Harvard. In retrospect, my father had good judgment.

Harvard Medical School

When I arrived at Harvard Medical School, I was very disappointed because I could not do any research. Resources were scarce because of the war, some of the better teachers were off in the army and some of the courses were duplicates of what I had in Princeton.

In the middle of Boston there is a large part of Charles River where people tend to frequently sail. Coming from a first class sailing team in Princeton, I started to spend twenty hours a week sailing on the Charles River. During that first year, my classmates voted me to be the most likely to flunk out. They were not aware of my prowess at procrastination.

At the end of the first year, the school finally let me do research and I gave up my sailing except for Sunday mornings since there were races on Sundays. At the races, there was a man about fifteen years older than me who I usually beat because I knew the sailing rules better than he did. The funny thing is he was my mentor during my two months of internal medicine at the Boston City Hospital. It was a bit embarrassing for me because here was a professor in medicine at Harvard, who I had been beating in sailing and now I had to learn from him.

Dissecting Bodies

Anatomy lectures were pretty dull, but dissection was alright once I got over the first few times. It got a lot more interesting as we got into dealing with actual human bodies. The people who ran the dormitory cafeteria were regularly notified when the freshmen class had to do dissections because on days that the freshman class would start dissecting, eating would be one fourth of the usual amount. Eating would return to regularity in two or three weeks. We worked in teams of four for each body. On the first day, each body was face down and we started dissecting on the skin in the back.

Toward the end of the course, my dissecting team let me try to very carefully dissect out the delicate spiral that was the cochlea, where hearing takes place. We called over our instructor to show him what I had done. Apparently he didn't know what the cochlea looked like. He took his tweezers, plucked the cochlea and destroyed it within a second. I was infuriated because it was so pretty and he had destroyed it.

One night, a classmate was going out to a party and he was known to drink too much when he went out. As a prank, we moved all the furniture from his room to the room above his on the third floor and then we took the furniture from the room on the third floor and moved it into his room. The classmates from the third floor went down to the lower room and were studying there when he came home. He came home staggering into his room and excused himself for entering. There was a bit of conversation; "Did you have a good time?" and so forth. He went out to the floor below and there were his classmates who lived there. After some whisper, he excused himself. He walked outside, came inside and walked to the second floor, went to the door and the same people were there. This went on for an hour until they finally told him, and then quickly restored the furniture to their original positions.

Marine Hospital

I do not remember where I lived during my first month or two in Boston, but soon after admission I found a job as an aid at the Marine Hospital, which was a mile north from the medical school and close to the Charles River. There were five other students there and we each earned our room and board in return for working on Friday evening, all day Saturday and Sunday till 5 pm. The patients were old, retired members of the Navy and also people that the Navy saved from sunken boats and naval ships. We made beds, put out meals, assisted patients with eating where needed, handed out medicines, bathed and shaved the men. It took three nurses to keep track of what we did and record it all in the chart every day. I had an efficient way of giving enemas. There were three stalls that were three feet wide and four feet long with three toilets in them and no doors. I could put men on stretchers and wheel them into the bathroom. I had three stalls there from which I could put a tube in the anus and pour water into their colons in a short time. The more fluid you put in, the more the bowels moved. Therefore they kept the enemas flowing in until it would start to come out, one right after the other. I would lift them up and put them right on the toilets. Then I would take the stretchers and bring in three more men. Their stretchers were in front of the occupied toilets where those on the toilets could see them. If the men on the toilets had not moved their bowels, they realized they had better move them immediately.

During the time we were at the Marine Hospital there was a big fire in Boston and 450 people at a popular night club (90% of the people there that night) were burned to death. We were asked to come help pull out the bodies. Another time, I had a man who had been rescued from shore where he had been thrown into the water from an accident. He had been there for several days and was covered with insects and also had a temperature of 104°. I put him in a shower, went in myself, sprayed him with insecticide, washed him off, dried him and had put him into his bed, all within ten minutes.

On Sunday afternoons, I had to clean and polish the long straight marble floor on the third floor. The polishing wheel was a whirling, flat, circular brush about three feet wide with a five foot long handle. When I pushed the handle down, the brush went to one side and when I lifted the handle up, the brush went to the opposite direction. Without looking at what I was doing I could make the brush go from one side to the other within three inches on each side, so while I was polishing, I would read Gray's Anatomy text book. When I came to the end of the corridor I would go straight down the whole hospital corridor with the brush up against the wall. There was always gossip in the hospital about the way I polished the corridor.

The director of the Marine Hospital had heard stories about how I cleaned the long corridor on the 3rd floor. He wanted to see for himself if it was true and one Sunday he came to the hospital and walked up to the third floor very quietly not making any noise that would indicate that somebody was walking up the stairs. He went up there successfully, opened the door, and found that the "legend" was true.

They Were Going to Shoot Me

Part way through the first year of medical school, almost everybody was drafted into the Army or Navy. The two or three, who were not, had major physical problems. It was a great relief financially since the military paid my Harvard tuition and provided a salary for food, housing, books and uniforms. I didn't have to work at the Marine Hospital anymore. My family didn't have to send me any money. At the same time that we were drafted, the army also took over the dormitory and assigned us to rooms, which we shared. I was assigned to a two man room with an honest, hardworking man from Framingham, Massachusetts who could not stand living with me. I did half as much studying as he did and I always obtained better grades and he would complain about it to his friends all the time.

When the army took over, they sent a junior first lieutenant to be in charge. It turned out that many of the current medical students attended Harvard College with that first lieutenant when they were all juniors. He had the same classes as he had had in Harvard College. He felt that he was sent to train us to be soldiers instead of learning to give help to injured or sick soldiers. He insisted that we wake up early in the morning to go marching. Whenever he met one of us, we had to salute him. We were enlisted men and he was an officer so he was superior to us. He wanted to make sure that we knew this, and because of this we were not very fond of him. One day, as he came into the dormitory and started to walk up the stairs, a bag of water "accidentally" fell out of the window two flights above the stairs and landed right in front of him. He rushed in to find out who spilled the water. Nobody knew or would admit to who it was. Everyone he spoke to was sure that nobody would ever deliberately do something like that. It must have been an accident. Someone must have left some water there and forgot about it

and it fell out. The next day, which was a Friday, everyone had to go to the large main auditorium late in the afternoon. There he swore at all of us and told us that everyone had to stay in their dormitory. Over the coming weekend, people could only go to the laboratories or offices of the school with permission from professors. No one could travel to the church or the synagogue or a hospital on Saturday or Sunday. No one could go to the pharmacy, a block and a half away. None of this went over too well.

I was to work in the Medical Department Office and I quickly grew bored of the monotony. Writing all the notes of everything that had transpired in English, I instead wrote all the notes in German. When the Captain saw what I had done, he came out of the building demanding, "Where's Seed?!" He said I ought to be shot. My punishment was having to type for two days.

The Principles of Army Warfare

Three of our colleagues who had dropped the water, had gone to the public library where they took out the book, *The Principles of Army Warfare*. Among the text there was a statement indicating that an officer must not swear at enlisted soldiers. It also explained what an enlisted man had to do to bring charges against an officer. No more than four soldiers could try this. They had to approach the officer's desk and get no closer than 48 inches, salute, present the charges, salute again, turn around and leave. Our colleagues did so and made sure that their uniforms were in perfect shape and their shoes were polished when they did. After that, they went to the newspapers in Boston and told them that they had presented charges against their commanding officer.

Meanwhile our officer called his superior, who was at the Harvard College across the Charles River in Cambridge. He sent the complaints to the army General in charge of all military operations in the North-Eastern part of the United States. The newspapers were calling to find out if it was true that the students at Harvard Medical School had presented charges against their commanding officer. The General called the Second Lieutenant in Cambridge, who had just received the charges thirty minutes earlier, and he replied with a soft timid voice "Yes, sir, just thirty minutes ago." The General said, "Well, get him out." It took ten days before they could replace him. The General called the newspapers and he told them that it was true. The students at Harvard Medical School had prepared charges against their officer, but asked them not to publish it, for the benefit of the US Army, at the time of war and the newspapers obliged.

Our replacement was Major Rosenberg, M.D. from the front lines in Europe. He wished he was back in Europe and the first thing he said was that there was not to be any marching, and there would be no restrictions on where we went. However, there were two things we had to do. One was to clean up the Army's part of the dormitory if he got news that there was going to be an inspection. The other was to run his office on

weekends and record messages and phone calls. Two thirds of the dormitory was for the Army and the other third was for the Navy. One day, late in the morning, the news came that there was going to be an inspection that afternoon and away we went. Everything out in the open was put in large military bags: Books, papers, pencils, shoes, socks, charts etc. We quickly carried them over into the Navy's part of the dormitory because we knew that the army had no right to inspect that area, and then we made all the beds. During the inspection, the Major was complemented on how neat the dormitory was kept. It didn't occur to the inspectors that there might be books, extra shoes, writing paper etc in a student's room. It took three days to get everything back in order. The Major received full credit from the military for how well everything looked.

Dormitory was Cleaned up

   Selection for manning the Major's office was done by random. On my turn, I thought it might be interesting to do everything in German. The Major came in on Monday morning and found that everything in the record was in German instead of English. He was in a rage. He rushed out of the office looking for me. Whenever he saw anybody, he asked them if they knew where I was. They would answer, "No, what is the problem?" He would tell them what I had done and said, "If I find him, I am going to have him shot" and he would go on his way. I heard about how he felt and stayed out of sight. Over and over again he got the same response. By 11:00 am he settled down and I had a friend tell him that I would be at the pharmacology lecture. He found me and told me that I should not do things like that or he would have to punish me. The punishment was to do two hours of typing this upcoming Saturday afternoon. That was sure better than being shot!

I Ate the Oyster

   I started doing research at the beginning of my second year. The first piece of work was to understand the purpose of the large amounts of acetylcholine in the cornea of the eye. I wanted to see what the amount was and how it was held there. To do this I went to the slaughterhouse in Boston where they killed cattle. I was stationed at the site where the heads came off and I dug out the eyes and carried them back to the laboratory at the Quadrangle at Harvard. In order to measure the acetylcholine concentration, I used the heart of an oyster. I went down to the waterfront in the bay of Boston and bought quality oysters. I took them back to the laboratory and carefully cut off the hinge of the oyster shell to get to the heart underneath. With extreme finesse, I took out the heart and put it in water that had the same salt concentration as the ocean did. One end of the heart was tied to a metal ring that served as an anchor and the other end was tied to a piece of very fine thread that was attached to a lever. When exposed to acetylcholine, the oyster's heart muscles contracts. The higher the concentration was the stronger the contraction. Before I started making the measurements, I stopped and ate the rest of the oyster. I felt a little guilty, but I didn't want to waste the oyster. I eat oysters in restaurants without any feeling of guilt, but then again, I don't cut out their hearts. Despite all of this work, nothing significant ever became of it.

In my third year, I had a two month session for internal medicine at the Boston City Hospital. The teacher in charge was the man that I was beating at sailboat racing on Sunday mornings. I wasn't working up to par during the first three days and he asked one of the residents, who was engaged in the teaching, to talk to me about it. He did and I promised to do better. The day he spoke to me, was the day I finished a piece of work I was doing about how variorum (a chemical) varied and I finished writing it up. I went to work full steam and about a week later, I heard him talking to another resident while they were on a stairway two floors below me. He said, "One of the things about these Harvard students is that when you talk to them, they really respond!" Several years later a surgeon from Harvard Medical School, who was then in the Surgeon General's office in Washington, DC, came to Boston to find physicians for the army's chemical warfare department. I recommended that same fellow who spoke about me on the stairwell. After a few years the war was over and one of the men from my group became the director of the Presbyterian Hospital in Chicago. He wanted to get rid of three surgeons who had been at the hospital for a long period of time. My father said to me that this person was being too hard on these three surgeons and that he should give them something else to do at the hospital instead of general surgery.

During my days in medical school, single males in their twenties were rare in the United States. Most of them were off somewhere in the army. The debutantes had a hard time finding men for their dances so they invited all the medical school students. Twenty or thirty of us would show up for these affairs. Half of us would dance with the women, while the other half would drink wine and eat sweets. After thirty minutes, the drinking and eating group would go on the floor and tell the dancing group that they could go back to the tables and the bars. Thirty minutes later there was another exchange and so this rotation went on during the evening. Some of the women at these affairs managed to find spouses. During one of these dances I drank too much. Recognizing this, I got on my bicycle and pedaled back to the dormitory as fast as I could, dropped into my bed and passed out.

Incidentally, our class was the last class at Harvard Medical School that only accepted men. After our class, women were allowed to be admitted to Harvard Medical School.

Mr. Seed "A First Class Sailor"

I owned a seven foot long dingy while I was in medical school, which I had anchored off a small raft across the street from Massachusetts Institute of Technology. The water was about ten feet deep and there was a ladder to the top of the wall where there was a lawn. In the winter, while the sailboat was out of the water, I kept it leaning against the back of the medical dormitory. One Sunday afternoon I was out with a date and we were fooling around a bit and we ended up capsizing the boat. As I was turning the boat upright, an eleven year old boy sailed over to help. And when he saw it was me, he said in a loud disappointed voice, "Mr. Seed, and you are a first class sailor?" It was easy getting the boat upright and to get my date back into the boat. We then sailed back over to the raft, up the ladder, bicycled home, showered and got into dry clothes. There was nothing I could do for the boy though; his respect for the senior sailors was lost.

My Classroom Mates

I had three roommates the last year and a half of Medical School: Gulio D'Angio, Joseph Miller, and Lester Tobin. Gulio (who we called Danny) had a striking career after he spent two years at a sanatorium in upstate New York because he suffered from tuberculosis. Once he was cured, he went back to school and became head of radiation therapy for cancer at the University of Pennsylvania in Philadelphia. Joe Miller practiced internal medicine for a number of years and later wanted to become a politician. He became a member of the Senate in the state of New Hampshire. Lester went to Florida and settled there and is still practicing internal medicine.

In school, when Joe Miller was studying psychology, he became enmeshed by Freud. Any time one made an error, Joe claimed it was due to some psychological problems. His repeated explanations were trying, to say the least. One day, he backed his car into a telephone pole and dented the rear end fender of his car. We let him have it. "Joe, what is it that made you damage your fender? Why did you have to bend your fender? You can tell us, Joe. We are your roommates. We understand these things. What had been bothering you when you damaged the fender? Really, Joe these things can be treated, just relax." On and on, after two days of this we never heard of anything about Freud's theories again.

In those days tuberculosis was very common; twenty percent of the class had evidence of exposure to tuberculosis on admission to the class and one hundred percent at graduation. In a class of one hundred students, usually one of those would get active tuberculosis. At the time, no drugs were available to treat it. The only treatment was rest at a sanatorium. In my class, two developed active tuberculosis. One was one of my three roommates. When we were being taught to do physical examinations, the emphasis was on recognizing the tuberculosis, which meant listening to the lung.

Psychiatry

My turn for learning psychiatry came in my third year of medical school. I had a patient to see, but no instructions on how to interview him. They hadn't given me any particular thoughts about how to handle the talk or if they didn't understand them. At any rate, I talked with this man and it became quite apparent to me what his problems were. He had become aware of the cause of his depression. As a result, soon after our meeting he tried to commit suicide.

The next time I came in, they told me to be careful about what I said and how I said it. I thought, "Okay I'll just talk about music." It turned out that the man was a homosexual and all his interests were buried in music. As a pianist, he tried to use his ability to play the piano to hide his problems. He also tried to commit suicide.

The third time my instructor came in, he said, "Don't interview anybody, just do what you want to do." So I went to play pool. While I was playing pool, along came a patient who was about my size and height who had been a medical student, he joined me in some games of pool. In his second year of medical school he had a major psychological breakdown, which interrupted his career. After playing pool with me, he went outside and tried to kill himself. He climbed up a high tree and it took a whole squad of people to get him down.

Finally, my instructor said to me, "From now on, when you come in, go straight to the library! Use the side door so nobody in this institution can see you in any manner, shape or form. You come in from the side door and go home at the end of the day from the same door quietly. Don't let anybody see you in the library and we'll give you an A+ in psychiatry."

A+ in Surgery

When I was a fourth year student in medical school, I was appointed to surgery training in the hospital because of one of the regular interns had become sick. My father was a professor of surgery and I knew what surgery was all about. I didn't want to waste time hanging on to retractors - tools to keep the wound open. On the first day, I had to talk to a man who was going to be operated on the following morning for gallstones. During my physical examination, I observed signs of diabetes in the back of his eyes. The next morning, while they were deciding who was going do surgery, I said to the chief resident, "What are you going to do about his diabetes?" He said, "Diabetes!" I said, "Yes;" and he thumbed through the chart. There should have been lab work, but there were not urinalysis results and no blood tests or anything. He then said, "What do you mean diabetes?" I told him to look in his eyes. He didn't have an ophthalmoscope (an instrument for looking into the eyes), since surgeons don't generally need to use one. I lent him mine to use. He looked in the patient's eyes and said, "What's that?" I said, "That's diabetes!" He said, "We'd better postpone this surgery a bit and get a medical consult." They did get the consult. It was three days before they had him in shape to operate on. The patient himself didn't know he had diabetes. So I offered to perform physicals, put in IV's, take histories, things that I liked doing. I didn't like the thought of just standing there holding retractors during surgery. Only once in the two to three months that I was there did I actually help at an operation. It was three o'clock in the morning, when nobody else was available, and I went in and held on to retractors. Through all of this work on IV's and histories and physicals I got an A+ in surgery.

Ran a Boat Ashore

In 1945 during my last month in medical school our group went out sailing with our dates in Boston Bay with a rented two masted, sixty foot boat. We started about 9:00 am and planned to be back by about 6:00 pm. We brought sandwiches, cookies and soft drinks. Around 2:00 pm a classmate who was at the helm wanted me to take over. I asked the classmate, "Where is that buoy over there on this map?" He pointed to a spot and I said, "What about the one over there?" He pointed to another spot and I took over the helm. Right then when I looked out over the water, the boat went aground. My classmates laughed and they gave me a hard time. Here I was the classmate who had the reputation of being the best sailor in the class and I ran the boat aground. The tide was running out so the boat was getting higher and higher and the water got lower and lower. The coast guard came over to see what happened. They left three of us to take care of the boat until the tide turned back in and that would not be until six o'clock in the morning. We went down inside the boat to see if there was any damage and we did not see any. In the morning the boat came afloat and we started to put up the sails when the coast guard appeared and said, "Put the sails down, we are towing you back to the dock." It was said in a very positive way. We did not protest.

Massachusetts General Hospital

During my internship I had two or three hours of sleep when I was on duty, and 8 hours of sleep on my days off. During that time I gained thirty pounds because there were no charges for food for the interns. We were paid $10.00 a month. They served meals at breakfast, noon, evening as well as 11:00 pm and 3:00 am. The meals were free only on my days of duty. We lived in a building that was attached to the hospital. Cleaning and laundry were taken care of. There was a room with a pool table in it. I was the champion pool player among the interns. During the nine months that I lived there I spent one Sunday afternoon sailing in the Charles River in a dinky six foot boat for two people. I was on the sailing team at Princeton University when I was a student and we were the National Champions. That Sunday was the only time I left the hospital. I loved what I was doing. It was a challenge to outwit some of the best minds in the country.

Poor solitary patients were still coming to Massachusetts General Hospital in 1945, when I came there as an intern. There was a long wide room that had sixteen beds, eight on each side separated from each other by curtains hanging from the ceiling. There was also a smaller room with six patients, three on each side also with curtains hanging from the ceiling to separate them. The beds were all numbered and the order in which the patients were seen by the doctors or interns was always the same. When the attending doctors came to see the patients and teach us the curtains were pulled aside. If the patient had a problem that seemed to be rheumatism or bone problem, the attending doctor would always want to know the patient's calcium level. All other laboratory results came the same day that the blood was drawn and was available when the attending doctor was talking to us. To avoid having the attending doctor ask us to order a calcium test, we would put the patients that might have bone or rheumatoid arthritis disease at the very end of the list of patients to be seen that day. We would then keep him occupied with the other patients by asking many questions about the patients and things that would interest him. After a while we would ask the doctor, "What is next?" When we advised him of the next patient, who would be the patient with bone or rheumatoid arthritis disease, he would already be too busy for the day. His reply would be, "I can't see him now, I have an appointment, I want him to be the first patient tomorrow." Our answer was, "Yes, sir." By that time we would have the calcium level and he would be seeing a problem of the kind that he likes. Our manipulation was no injury to the patient. If the next patient might have arthritis, he or she would not have been seen until the beginning of the next day.

Some of the patients we saw were private patients of the attending doctors. We took their histories and did their examinations, but we were not permitted to order any laboratory tests. However, they didn't say we couldn't do the laboratory tests ourselves. So we did the test ourselves, but did not put that into the patients' charts and we were always right. The attending doctors would read the charges and then tell us that we had overlooked some possibilities. We would explain why we thought it was thus and so, but did not mention our own lab work. One time a man came in with pus coming from his rib bone on the side of his chest. We took a look at the pus under the microscope and that pus was loaded with actinomycets, a fungus. When the attending came in to see his patient the next day he discussed with us what diseases he might have, but he didn't comment about the rib. Then he asked us what we thought it was and we said fungus infection of the third rib. There is pus coming out of the rib. He then said in a very strong, stern voice, "One day you boys are going to make a mistake, I hope I am here to see it!"

One time a doctor admitted a patient to the separate smaller unit at the Massachusetts General Hospital, which was used for the wealthier patients. The patient was an eighty-three year old man who was admitted at nine o'clock in the morning on a Friday. He was a little uncomfortable. His wife had died five years before. He had hired a woman to take care of him and the house. The woman had taken three days off that weekend. The doctor thought he did not need a work up. The doctor told me that everything was all right and that the patient was just a little tired that Friday morning. I felt that being in the hospital for a little rest and care; he really ought to have a work up, just because he was in the hospital, even if nothing was wrong. By Friday at noon time, I was sure he had pneumonia and I ordered a chest x-ray. His doctor was not available that morning and I had gone ahead without his permission. I started doing blood work, culture, started antibiotics and so on. I kept asking for permission from the regular doctor; however the doctor was not responding. I was seeing the patient hourly. Saturday morning I did a second chest x-ray. Finally on Sunday night I got permission to take the x-rays. On Monday morning his lungs were a little better. His regular doctor came in to see him. He looked at his patient, looked at his chart and did a brief examination. He said to me, "Very good, and the next time I send in patients, you take care of them and just let me know how they are."

One evening when I was on duty at the emergency room of the Massachusetts General Hospital, a woman was brought in by on of the routine Massachusetts police officers from central Boston. She had been wandering around in the area and nobody knew who she was. She would talk to no one. There was no sign of injury. She had a purse; however it did not contain any identification. She walked, but would not talk. She wasn't happy or sad, she didn't cry, she had a flat looking face. She drank water. She sat down when she was asked to do so. A physical exam didn't reveal anything. She had a vertical 12 inch scar four to six months old in the middle of the abdomen. She was about five feet tall and she was standing quietly and still. She showed no emotion. Her clothing showed no signs of where they were made; because it turned out they were made at the mental asylum where she lived. The asylum locally manufactured items all made with no labels. But none of us were thinking about that source and what that meant. It turned out at the end that she had escaped from her mental asylum. While I was trying to figure out who she was, I decided to call hospitals in the area to find out if they had done any surgery that would have left her with the scar on her abdomen. The first three calls were negative. On calling the fourth hospital, the Boston City Hospital, I also received a negative response. The resident had indicated no to me, but then I added some more information about her, the way she looked, the way she acted and the way she talked. With that additional information the Boston City Hospital resident remembered her. I then called the asylum and indentified her. The people from the asylum said they would take her in the morning the following day to bring her back. That morning I thought we should check to see if she had any metal links in her stomach before she left our hospital. I asked radiology to have an x-ray to check for metal links in her abdomen. She was in the x-ray department and she was quite upset. They put her on the x-ray table. The radiologist was having some trouble with her and a medical intern happened to be going by and offered to help keep her lying at the proper position. One of the medical interns was also there and volunteered to push the button for the x-ray table she was lying on. The intern had her head up a little bit. The one medical intern kept pushing the button. The radiologist was asking him to stop, but the intern didn't quite understand. She ended upright, but attached to the table by her head, chest, abdomen and lap. The radiologist told the intern to slow it down, he pushed the wrong button. He told him to strap her in better. The patient was getting more and more upset by this. After twenty minutes, she was getting very high. The radiologist was infuriated because the table had passed the normal level. The radiologist was angry and asked the hospital's floor cleaner to push the buttons. The patient was now shouting and screaming. They had her tied flat on the table. Right then the people came from the asylum to bring her back, while she was all strapped down on the table. Once she was back at the asylum, she told the story about what had happened to her at the Massachusetts General Hospital, but nobody believed her.

Life at the Massachusetts General Hospital

In the first month of my internship, I had a patient who was a man who had an infection of one of the valves of the heart. It is a very serious infection and nobody had ever survived it. I felt that the penicillin might cure him. My attending, who happened to be the Chairman of Medicine Department, said that the penicillin has been tried and it doesn't work. I said, "But I don't think they had given enough penicillin." He said, "We have already tried and it doesn't work, forget about it." So I didn't say anything to him, but I went ahead and determined the lowest concentration of penicillin that would kill the bacteria that was damaging the heart. Then I calculated how much of that concentration of penicillin would be needed to be given intravenously steadily for a twenty four hour period. It turned out that the amount required would cost $100 a day. I thought that the penicillin would have to be given continually for fifteen days to be successful. This meant a total of $1,500. The man ran a radio repair shop, and he had a wife and two children. His annual income was about $4,000. It was not possible for him to be able to pay for the penicillin. The other intern went with me (there were always two interns on duty at any service) to see if the United Jewish Appeal could give us the money needed to buy the penicillin for this patient. They agreed to give us the money. Then we went back to our attending and told him that the United Jewish Appeal had agreed to give us the $1,500 to buy the penicillin. He said, "Go ahead and waste the time and the money of the United Jewish Appeal." We gave the patient the penicillin and he was the first person to ever survive that type of infection. Our attending physician, who was the Chairman of the Department of Medicine, called all the major medical schools across the country and told them this infection could be cured. He said, "My interns have just cured it, Subacute Bacterial Endocarditis, with penicillin". He then told them how to do it. This was in July of 1945.

Life in the Army

During my internship at the Massachusetts General Hospital from 1945 to 1946, a surgical professor from Harvard Medical School had gone to the army medical department for the war, and returned to speak with the chairman of the department of medicine to find out if anyone in the army was interested in Pharmacology. The first thing he did was to come to the Medical Department of Harvard Medical School, where the chairman of medicine knew of my interest in Pharmacology, so he told him about me.

The chairman was from the office of the Surgeon General of the army in Washington, DC. He was sent to find some physicians for the Army Chemical Warfare Department. He had interviewed me and then asked me if I knew of anybody else that would be interested. So I listed five of my classmates, plus six from the class ahead of me that I thought would be the best to work with, in addition to the one he selected from Harvard. That meant there were twelve people from Harvard, two from John Hopkins and two from Cornell. We became a tight group of sixteen. After the war was over, one of the members of our group became the head of medicine at the Presbyterian Hospital in Chicago and didn't know that his professor of anatomy was my father. My father was a surgeon and that was his main focus of work. However, because he needed to earn additional money he did work as a professor of anatomy as well.

Ben Landing was my closest friend . He was a physician from Cornell University. We lived in the same room, and founded a journal which we called the INTERN. It only lasted two issues because of the war. This was one of the dramatic experiences I had. During the war I roomed together with Ben Landing in the same building as the other officers. Ben and I felt it was our duty to awaken all the officers so they could be sure to get to the mess hall in time for the morning meal. It was very hard to get Robert Murphy out of bed; therefore we decided to try something a little ingenious. Juicy Fruit chewing gum smelled just the same as one of the nerve gases. So we decided to go into his room to place one stick of it underneath his pillow and then stood back in the corner of his room. We watched him sniffing and he reached up with his eyes still closed and he grabbed his gas mask, put it on, jumped out of bed and opened his eyes as he ran out of the building. Although he had been in a sound, deep sleep, he did not fumble for a minute; he knew exactly where his gas mask was in the room. All of us knew where our gas masks were all the time. He got dressed and started to leave the room. As he was leaving the building he noticed that back in the room there were two men that were not wearing gas masks. It was Ben Landing and I. He was mad. We said, "But Robert, we got you out of bed."

Before I could go to the Army Chemical Warfare Center I had to go through nine months of training on how to work on taking care of the soldiers injured in battles. This was done at an Army Center near San Antonio, Texas. The summer there was very hot and very dry. Most of the teaching was done sitting in a small stadium and the seats were generally so hot that one had to stand and make a shadow over the seat before you could sit. Otherwise it was a burning hot seat. The temperature outside was about 110°. It was very unpleasant. In that time of the year in town, there were swimming pools; however due to the polio epidemic people were not allowed in the pools.

I remember one afternoon, there was a truck, and they were giving instructions of where all the instruments are supposed to go in the truck. Instructions of what to do in case groups of people might be injured. It was very tiring and the sun was very unpleasant. In the evenings we lived in a large four floor building that could house 1,000 people. We were a group of 780. Beds were covered with sheets. We went into the shower to cool down before going to sleep, and then 30 to 50 minutes later we took a shower again to cool down and went back to sleep and we did this three or four times a night. We had meals that were adequate. The lectures were dull. They did examinations after the training, testing our memory. Then they thought we should march and learn how to salute officers, the same as the regular soldiers did. It was the time of the 4th of July and they had a number of contests; one of which was a marching contest. A group of forty of our physicians decided to enter the contest and they won it. The day after the contest they still had to march across the street. They shouted as we marched, "Four – four – two – one;" then, "Two – two – one – one," and so on. We were not in order. The fellow who was in charge said, "I take offense to that!" He did not know that one of his group had won the marching contest the day before; to him the group appeared very casual. After everyone was past the road they had to stand in a long group, but it was very casual. As a result he asked one of the group to come forward to direct the group. The man came out and said, "March forward!" Everyone was in order and marching all in the same order. After ten feet he said, "Column left!" They did so immediately. After about ten more feet the soldier who was in charge said, "Halt! He then said, "This is an insult." He took over and started them in on a regular manner.

He didn't realize the tallest ones were the first and the shortest ones were the last. After a while the smallest faked that he was injured and was asking for help. The soldiers around him got into helping him after marching 100 yards. The officer in charge came over to see what had happened. He didn't know what was going on. When he got there he called out to halt, but the tall doctors were too far ahead to be heard. They had gone over a steel fence. The tallest had gradually increased their speed and were running and ran over the steel fence into a corn field.

Halfway through the march, each group of six doctors had been given instructions as to where the next point was posted. It was getting dark and one could hear splashing.

People were wondering where they were. Now they had seven hundred doctors (which was 75% of all physicians in the United States) lost somewhere in the swamp. They called in the Air Force and the planes came out. Flares were all over the swamp. The whole sky was covered. Loud instructions were given out. By three o'clock in the morning they had found all of the doctors.

My next assignment was the laboratory in Brook Hospital because my background was laboratory work. I had different ideas on how to do things. So they sent me to the laboratory for twelve days. Then they sent me to the rehabilitation center to take care of the injured soldiers that remained in the center. The routine was to see the soldiers that wanted to be seen in the morning at the clinic. It took two to three hours. The soldiers came down only if they wanted to be seen. I asked them how they were doing. I said that I wanted to see every soldier in the place, whether they wanted to be seen or not. For the rest of the day, I wanted to see one at a time. I wanted to find out what their problems were. One soldier had trouble walking around. He had broken a bone in the thigh. It won't heal if he keeps moving. I sent him back to the Brook Hospital. The doctors there were mad about receiving my nasty notes about the treatment for this patient. They were happy to get rid of me after a while. They had not yet made a decision about what I would be doing next, so they sent me home for a month.

While I was waiting in my home in Chicago for the order to go to the Army Medical Center, I had supper on Thursday evenings with James Arnold. He was one of my friends from the group in Princeton and he was working at the University of Chicago. He was studying for a PhD in Biochemistry and was working on the side for a project on the Atom Bomb. My new orders came at the end of the month to report to the Army Chemical Center testing grounds below the Great Salt Lake. My order was to go with Dr. Robert Murphy, another research physician. Dr. Murphy wanted to drive there and I agreed, so he stopped in Oak Park, Illinois to pick me up. When we started off at eight o'clock in the morning, he had an attitude of being very superior to me. He criticized me about my intelligence. This continued steadily until he made a critical comment and I finally responded. This resulted in us becoming very good friends. We drove through Salt Lake City, then to Tooele, and then Clover. At Clover there was only one gasoline station and four houses. We left the gasoline station and went straight out on that road out of town. After a few hours there were no poles for electric wires, no signs of activity, no houses; only a straight paved road and nothing else. On we went for another thirty miles and then we started to go up the east side of the Wasatch Mountain Range. We didn't see a house or any civilization. We were going south and west. We were driving over the mountain. After zigzagging through, we were driving carefully suddenly we saw a big sign with one foot tall letters that read: WATCH OUT FOR CHILDREN. We went further and finally could see in the distance some houses forty miles to the west. We had found the Army Medical Center where testing was to be done. It was called Great Salt Lake Desert. We drove over to the desert test area and training range, which had no public access. They let us use the house for travelers. The first thing we did out there was clean up the laboratory and put it together so that we could do some real work. The officer in charge criticized Murphy for smoking a cigarette. He came over the next day to see what we had done. The officer was criticizing what we were doing, even though he didn't have a good score in college. He reprimanded us just one time. He had no power over us. The orders for us to work on Chemical Warfare came from Washington DC, not from the Army Chemical Center.

We made some bombs and we took them out into one of the testing areas which was a long way from where our lab was located. We were wearing our gas masks. We had to do monitoring of what happened to the fuel chemicals: what was left, how fast etc. The other soldiers at Dugway came out to see. They were 1,000 feet away watching what we did. The bomb was set fifteen feet behind a pile of ground fifteen feet high by fifteen feet thick. We were standing about sixty feet back from the pile.

After the bomb testing, Murphy and I went up to see a mountain that was made of rocks that had areas that were similar to diamonds. This was a one day trip. At the mountain, we picked up a number of samples and took them back. In getting out to the mountain, we stopped three times to urinate. Two months later I was up in a plane doing bombing tests. I saw the marks on the surface of the desert of where we had urinated, along the car tracks.

There was a small area in the desert where the regular soldiers and their families lived. Some of the soldiers had their families with them, and they had dogs, the dogs might come out in the steps of their house at night. The dogs didn't go very far because of the coyotes around the camp. They would be barking from thirty feet away and running around. Occasionally the dogs went too far from the houses and were eaten by coyotes, but it was rare. We could hear the coyotes at night time. It was not a good idea to be outside at nighttime because of the coyotes.

After three weeks at the Army Chemical Warfare Center, we started our way back, Robin and I stopped at all the major, famous sites in the west: Grand Canyon National Park, Petrified National Park, Dinosaur National Park, Bryce Canyon National Park, Zion National Park, Rocky Mountain National Park, the famous bat cave in Texas. Murphy had a girlfriend who lived in Houston, Texas. I went to a restaurant and ate by myself so they could have some time alone. After that it was a non-stop drive to Murphy's family estate in the Shenandoah area of Virginia.

Chemical Warfare

In the laboratory, at the Army Chemical Warfare Center where I worked, there was a hood three feet off the floor, three feet wide, three feet tall and two feet deep with a glass front that could be easily lifted up and pulled down. In the back at the top there was a six inch wide exhaust pipe which was active all the time. The purpose of a hood is to contain the effects of experiments for the safety of the scientist. It was a place to work with the most toxic stuff there is.

One day I tried to do an interesting thing with a petri dish. I took one and put in some water and added a small amount of the Tabun nerve gas. Then I pulled down the glass. There was an opening a quarter of an inch high and left it alone for the night without the covering. When I came in the morning the petri dish was surrounded by dead roaches in a water drop configuration. No live roaches touched the petri dish. Directly next to the petri dish, the roaches were piled five to six high. Slightly further out from the dish the pile of dead roaches was down to three or four roaches. The further away from the dish, the pile of dead roaches was lower and lower.

In the laboratory of the Chemical Warfare Research Department, there were a large number of cockroaches. There was an entomological division which was growing cockroaches. The spinal cord of the cockroach was the best thing for studying how nerve gas works. The roach nerve is large, long and easy to get to. It is just under the thick, transparent shell of the back of the roach. When one is breeding cockroaches, it is very hard to prevent escapes. Some of them are bound to escape; in addition there may be some wild cockroaches. I had a desk in the office with two other doctors, mine being in the middle of the three. We all had roaches in and around our desks. I did not like to see a cockroach come out when I opened up my drawer, so I went outside and caught a praying mantis. I put a very fine black thread around the neck of the praying mantis. The other end of the thread was tied down to the top of the middle of my desk. From there the praying mantis could roam around and pick up roaches and eat them throughout the night and day. The eating of the cockroaches by the praying mantis was pretty noisy, since they start by tearing off the back of the roach. In three days my desk was free of roaches. Off and on, I would go over to the entomological division and get some roaches for my praying mantis. I never used insecticides. If my praying mantis was getting thin, I would go and get some food for it: cockroaches.

New Gas Weapon

One day, I wanted to do a test trial on a new gas weapon, but before doing it I wanted to see where the smoke of this trial would go. Would it go in the direction where people might be exposed? Was a change in direction likely? How much of the contents might go up or down in the air, etc? I set off a bomb containing a strong white powder to test wherever the contents might go. I went outside to see where the dense white smoke was going. It turned out that the people in a far part of the building, one hundred feet diagonally from where I currently was, were being exposed. The smoke was coming out of the laboratory hoods, directly into their rooms, instead of going outside. The building's ventilation system had been poorly designed. If the wind was blowing in a certain direction this could happen. The people who were working in that part of the building had been complaining off and on about being exposed to the nerve gas, but all their complaints were ignored. The administration accused them of simply being paranoid. I was occasionally working with nerve gas under my hood and I was never aware of the complaints in that part of the laboratory. After that, they found that the people were right and finally, after a long time, they corrected the error.

Salute the General

When a general's car goes by it has a little red flag on the top of the fender on the left side. Anybody with the rank less than the general's is expected to salute the car when the general is in it. None of us in our group of lieutenants knew about the regulation and one received an official reprimand for not saluting the general's car. We took that reprimand very lightly and decided it would be interesting to start a contest to see who could obtain the most reprimands. I "lost" as I only received nineteen reprimands! One of my friends received twenty-three. After a while, the general who had been in the army for five or six years decided to go to our boss, a physician, and he gave us carte blanche to do anything we wanted in the line of research. We liked him and we completed a lot of good research. The general said there were some things that we absolutely had to do in the army and military, namely salute the general and higher officers or we would receive an official reprimand.

However, since we were directly controlled by Washington, DC and not the military, the general really had no authority over us. Because of this, we enjoyed giving the general a tough time since he insisted on giving us official reprimands. We sent a request to the Inspector General's department to send somebody down to inspect the substandard conditions of the facilities. The general was in hot water for nine months trying to get them fixed up. Then, we condemned the officer's mess and he was then in trouble for the next six months. Finally, we brought to the attention of Washington, DC that the officer's club was not being properly managed. Whenever there was a chance that he was doing something wrong, we spotted it. It was continuous.

There was one hospital at the Army Chemical Warfare division where we were located. There was only one doctor at this station. He was a trained physician in the army. He saw all the army soldiers and their families for their medical problems. This doctor would see patients from eight o'clock in the morning till five o'clock in the evening during the week. He was not available on weekends or holidays. On those days a trained soldier would take over. If the problem was a serious one, the patient was sent to another hospital. On our normal hours, we occasionally gave some medical care that was not covered by the station physician. When we arrived we took care of all the medical problems that were unusual and that the station physician could not handle.

After a while it occurred to me that the doctor was incompetent and decided to send a letter to the Army Medical Center in Washington, DC explaining what was going on at our Chemical Warfare Center. They sent two doctors to evaluate the current station physician. After that, they came to see me and told me that they did find that he was incompetent. They said they were going to send him to Korea, because they did not feel he would cause any serious problems working in Korea. The station general was a good friend of the incompetent doctor. The general has the authority to counter order on the post, but did not have the authority to order us off the post. The incompetent doctor stayed. One day the general became really ill and the incompetent doctor took care of him. He progressively got sicker and sicker. The doctor made five serious mistakes in a row. We were not able to treat the general and he eventually died at the center's hospital.

Chemical Warfare Error

One weekend when I was covering the station hospital, a fellow came in rubbing his eyes. I thought that was unusual, therefore I took a history and found out later they were decontaminating mustard gas containers. The cleansing process was designed for only fifteen pounds of mustard gas. However they were not doing fifteen pounds, they were instead doing one hundred and fifty pounds using the same procedure. Then, they pushed mustard gas out the top and over the landscape. We had a lot of patients come in with mustard gas burns in their eyes. When the first fellow came into the station hospital and I took his history, I couldn't figure out what was happening. Then a second fellow came in rubbing his eyes. I knew something was going on. Upon questioning, I found there was a major who was in charge of this building's chemical operation. I called him up and said, "Major, you have got mustard gas loose in building #664." He said, "That is impossible!" Just then a third fellow came in rubbing his eyes. I said to the major, "I've got three people over here with vapor burns in their eyes and you have to look into it." The major responded, "I don't have to look into anything. It's impossible." I said, "Well, if that is impossible, then you must have a brand new type of agent over there and you have to come over and find out what it is." I continued by saying, "Look, I am the Medical Officer of the Day. I am going to have to call up the general and tell him that you are proceeding with this operation against the advice of the Medical Officer of the Day." He finally conceded and went over to investigate. There were fifty-six men in that shift. They all came over to the hospital to be treated. The major then began telling the men that I am giving them the wrong treatment and not to follow my advice. He told them they would go blind if they followed my instructions. I told the major that we do not do it that way anymore, but he was very persistent. I finally said, "Major, I am the Medical Officer of the Day on these grounds. That includes the entire site, the walkway over there, the fence along there, the bushes along the side and the road out front! Now get out! That is an order! Leave. And if you do not leave, I will have you shot. This is a time of war. This is an official order to get off the premises of the hospital." After that, he then told his friends in chemical warfare, "Dr. Seed is treating all those people at the hospital incorrectly. Let's get him. We will have a trial."

They did have an official trial against me for incompetence in doing my work. They had court stenographers there taking notes. They swore me in and I took an oath. Then they asked me questions for an hour and half. I became tired of answering the questions, so I started to make accusations against each of the five Chemical Warfare colonels, who were my judges. They were not medical men who were trying me for improper medical care. I wrote down, for each of the five separate colonels, an episode where they showed incompetence and where men got poisoned. This document contained the five episodes, one for each of them. The next day, they had my boss come in to testify. He testified that I did everything correctly. He also had brought with him one of the latest manuals in treating gas casualties and pointed out that it was written by Lt. Campbell and Lt. Seed. This was an official document of the army on how to treat chemical warfare burns and accidents. They were not very happy in seeing this. They asked the Surgeon General from Washington, DC to send somebody down to testify. This man did not know anything about mustard gas and found a manual, which was only four months old and he studied it very carefully. After they swore him in, he testified everything right straight out of the manual that I co-wrote. His testimony too was no good for them! They asked the Major General of Chemical Warfare to send someone else down. This one also did not know much about the subject. So he scurried around and found this same manual and studied it carefully. They swore him in and he gave his testimony word for word from the manual. So then, they went to Columbia University, John Hopkins University and Yale University and asked them all to testify about the burns. All three universities had the same response: "Why don't you just ask Dr. Seed to testify, he knows more about that subject than anyone else." The judges couldn't find anybody in the United States who would testify against me! Therefore they had no choice, but to acquit me!

Whenever there is a trial the minutes go to the Inspector General's department to be read over. Hearing the accusations I made against these five colonels, the inspector general could not just ignore them. They began to look over other things that these colonels have done and found out that they had made other mistakes as well. So they conducted an investigation to find out if I am correct. Each one of the colonels received an official reprimand, which in turn blocked all further promotions. Their careers in the army were now over!

Nerve Gas is Loose

A year later, two men were making nerve gas while dressed in impervious clothing. It was perfectly safe for them to do this. After each batch they would empty it into a big container. There was one valve for putting in new batches and another valve for cleaning it out. Unfortunately the two valves were very close together. One day, after making a batch, they inadvertently turned the wrong valve and accidentally dumped twenty-five pounds of nerve gas into a nearby swamp, close to the army center, just about two and half miles away where the Corning Company had a manufacturing plant. A secretary at the Corning Plant called up the research lab and reached me by accident. She gave me a perfect description of early nerve gas poisoning. She said to me, "Everything is getting dark around here. It is strange, the sun is out, and it's getting dark." Nerve gas constricts the pupils in the eyes; hence everything gets dark. I did not ask anything. I knew nerve gas was loose. I assured her that we would be right over. I picked up the phone and called my colleagues. I said, "Hey gang let's go! They have nerve gas loose in the Corning Plant." I said, "I am going over right now. Get two ambulances and I will meet you down there." All sixteen of us dropped what we were doing, grabbed our gas masks and out we went. It was nerve gas alright. All the people were evacuated from the area. Some of them required medical treatment.

It was a lovely day in April with a gentle breeze blowing off the Chesapeake Bay causing the gas to be carried at least two and a half miles – enough to reach US Highway 40, which was the western border of the US Army Chemical Warfare site. We then checked the potential of poisoning two and half miles in all directions from where we were. One of us was on each side of the highway in order to pull people off the side of the highway to check them. Finally the breeze blew away the nerve gas. We did not lose anybody during this second incident, but we came close.

There was another incident after nerve gas got loose. It was not my fault, but I handled the situation. A young captain came looking into the matter. He went to the office of the colonel, who had been through the previous episodes. The young captain demanded that the person in charge of this third nerve gas poisoning incident should be court marshaled. The colonel responded, "I want you to erase all traces of who was on the site."

After things had settled down a man who had a mild exposure to nerve gas took out a cigarette. He took about two puffs and dropped to the ground unconscious. I gave him an injection of atropine and he became conscious right away. He was cautioned about smoking for the next month. The effect of nerve gas is made worse with the addition of nicotine. No gas abolishes cholinesterase and it takes a month for the body to completely replenish it.

If one wants to safely stop smoking, the patient comes in is given a small amount of nerve gas every two weeks. The patient will find it difficult to combine smoking with cholinesterase.

Meeting My Wife

After the big military affairs were over, a classmate of mine and I were double dating. After four dates I stopped seeing the woman I was dating. She was a student at Radcliff, a women's college, which was a part of Harvard College. However, at the time it was not officially recognized as part of Harvard. My classmate and his date asked me why I stopped dating her, since they had seen no outward signs of disagreements between us. I told them that if I keep on dating her I will end up marrying her, and she was not very bright. I wanted to have bright children and the best way to have bright children is to have a bright wife. I learned twenty-eight years later that she was an alcoholic. I was right about her.

My mother had always emphasized to me, her first born child, the importance of marrying a bright woman, which I ultimately did and was successful. The woman I did marry had a Master's degree in Biology from Harvard. She became the first female teacher at Northwestern University. She taught a class in Biology for two years and was also a research associate at Massachusetts Institute of Technology. Her name was Pauline (but she liked to be called Polly) and she met my criteria alright!

The army had a program for preservation of fabrics that had been given to Polly. Polly became the person in charge of that program. My roommate in the army, Ben Landing was in the same group as Polly. She took a chemistry course that was offered at the Army Chemical Center, and she was the top student in that course of thirty people.

Polly went to public elementary school; and after that she went to high school in Wellesley, Massachusetts and then to The Catholic Regis College. Her biology teacher was a nun whom she admired. Polly graduated from Catholic Regis College in 1935. After graduating, she went to Harvard University. She spent two summers doing research with the famous water studies at Waquoite Bay Woods Hole, Massachusetts. She graduated from Harvard in 1936.

Polly's father was an automobile dealer in a suburb of Boston called Wellesley. Polly had a brother who served in the United States Army during World War II. During the war, he was seriously injured in one of his knees. He joined the Unites States Post Office workers and earned his way to become Head of the Post Office for all of Boston, Massachusetts. He started working in the Wellesley Post Office, the same city where he, his sister and his mother lived. He and his mother died in that same house, many years later. He was gifted in working with mail men; as a result he was awarded year after year. In the end he was in charge of all the mail in Boston, Massachusetts. He died of cancer of the throat. Polly stayed with him for four days of each week for the last four weeks of his life. When there was no one else there with him he was anxious and afraid. The house was given to Polly after he died. After Polly's death, I eventually sold the house.

Sailing

One of my friends in the army, Van Aimee, had a date to go sailing on Robin Murphy's thirty-five foot yacht that was anchored off the dock right in front of the Army's Officer Club. Van Aimee was one of the sixteen doctors in the Army Chemical Warfare center. He had a date but the date's mother insisted that another woman be present because they were going to be on the boat. So he called me because he knew I was an accomplished sailor. However, all the women I knew were busy. My roommate, Ben Landing, suggested that I should ask the Sullivan woman. So I asked her if she would like to go sailing on a Sunday afternoon. She agreed to come along. After we got the boat under way; I went to the front end of the boat where I fell asleep. When it was time to go to the back so we could anchor, my friend said, "Go ahead; let's wake him up." He had my date and his date to keep him busy and to talk with while he was sailing and I was sleeping. Fortunately, that Sullivan woman (Polly) was not too upset.

We were going to go sailing the next weekend as well and I asked her if she would like to go sailing again. She agreed. This time there were three doctors with dates, Robin, Van and I. Polly came along as my date. Typically, we would leave the Army Chemical Warfare Center on Friday afternoon and sail off to some place on the Eastern Shore of Chesapeake Bay, where we had ordered rooms for the girls. We would give them supper and drop them off where they had admission, leave them on shore to stay in the rooms, while we slept on the boat. In the morning the girls would rejoin us on the boat and off we would go sailing. All meals were aboard the boat. I was the cook for the all the sailing trips until they ended in the last of October.

On one of our trips, it was about nine or ten o'clock at night, we were still sailing through the bay. We hadn't reached the spot where we had called ahead for the rooms for the girls. Around 11:30 pm we finally reached the spot. It was very dark and Robin was below deck calculating the movement of the boat due to the tide and the effects of the ocean. We were casually sailing and all of sudden Van yelled. He had good reason to yell, since we missed hitting a big ocean buoy by about a yard. We finally pulled up to the shore and anchored, sent the girls inside and Robin, Van and I slept on board, as usual. We woke up in the morning and I set out the meals for the girls and us. As we were leaving a few of the other motor boatmen started to ask us, "When did you guys come in? We didn't hear you." And we replied, "We sailed in. Not motored in."

In the fall Ben Landing and I were both taking evening classes at Johns Hopkins University while we were stationed thirty miles north of Baltimore. When I was in Princeton, I said I would never waste my time taking liberal arts courses. Well, I changed my mind and took some evening classes learning liberal arts. So, now I wanted to get those liberal art classes in whenever I could. While I was taking a course in Philosophy, Ben took a class on Irish literature. He had an Irish background and he already had taken two years of Irish Literature at Harvard University so now he knew more about the ancient Irish Literature. The teacher was in his third year of teaching Irish literature

The apartment where Polly lived was about two blocks from where I had class. So I'd go over there when class was over and asked if she'd like to come out and have ice cream with me. Every time I had class, I would spend a short evening with Polly. After that I would meet with Ben Landing and the two of us would go back to the army again.

After a year and a half of going to class, I asked Polly if she'd like to marry me. She hesitated for a month, especially since she had even previously considered being a nun. After she agreed to marry me, she introduced me to some Jesuit priests. I was impressed with what they taught me. I did some reading. She had attended a Catholic college and half of her undergraduate teaching was in Catholic schools. When we decided to get married, she said, "If we have children, they have to be brought up Catholic." I realized that raising children as Catholics was important to her. The thought of the children following her faith did not bother me at all. Polly and I had an agreement that we would have four children two years apart. We had sex for the first time on the night we were married and she became pregnant then.

At the marriage ceremony, my father said to me, "I don't give a damn about you, but I don't want a bunch of stupid Catholic grandchildren." It did not bother me. My father apologized twenty-seven years later for saying that about stupid Catholic grandchildren. His grandchildren were not stupid at all; they were all brighter than any of his colleagues' grandchildren.

Our Wedding Announcement

Miss Pauline F. Sullivan Bride of Dr. John Seed

At three o'clock, the wedding ceremony will be performed at St. Ingatius Church, Baltimore, Maryland on November 20, 1948 Miss Pauline F. Sullivan became the bride of Dr. John Cathro Seed of Baltimore. The Rev. John F. Dustan S.J. officiated. The bride is the daughter of Mrs. Francis J. Sullivan of Wellesley Hills and the late Mr. Sullivan, while Dr. Seed is the son of Dr. and Mrs. Lindon Seed of Chicago, Illinois.

Miss Sullivan, given in marriage by her brother, Mr. Francis S. Sullivan of Wellesley Hills, wore a wedding gown of ivory satin, fashioned with sweetheart neckline, long sleeves and train. Her finger-tip veil was caught to a band of orange blossoms and she carried a white prayer book adorned with two white orchids and streamers. The maid-of-honor, Miss Katherine Hastings of Hartford, Connecticut was dressed in light blue satin and carried an arm bouquet of red roses. Mrs. Sullivan, the bride's mother, wore forest green velvet with a corsage of purple orchids and the groom's mother, Mrs. Seed, wore gold colored lame with a purple orchid corsage. Dr. Benjamin Landing, who was a classmate of the groom at Harvard Medical School, served as best man. Ushers were Dr. Van Aimee of Philadelphia and Dr. James MacMurphy of New York City. Nearly one hundred guests attended the reception in the Oval Room of the Hotel Stafford in Baltimore after the ceremony.

The bride graduated from Wellesley High school and Regis College, and received her M.A. degree in mycology from Radcliffe College. For three years she was director of research at the Chemical Research Laboratory, Edgewood, Maryland. Dr. Seed, a graduate of Princeton University and Harvard Medical School, served four years with the Medical Division of the US Army. He was doing research in pharmacology at Johns Hopkins Hospital. The couple made their home in Baltimore after a two week wedding trip to the coast of upper Florida.

After The Wedding

Shortly after the wedding I took on a civilian position at the Chemical Warfare center supervising ten people in the development of new weapons. Polly and I went house hunting. It was fun. Since the military had maps of all the land nearby taken from an airplane 10,000 feet in the air and they had the ability to enhance the view so that license plates on cars were clearly readable, we had access to all of this. One particular plot of land looked interesting, but every time we went out to look at it, we couldn't find it. I finally got out of the car and walked around the road. After plodding through dense brush, along a dirt path I came to a house about a hundred yards in. It looked like an abandoned house. There was a partial fence. It was in such poor condition it was unsellable. We came across a very old white haired man who lived there. On the second floor there was a hole on the floor that you could see through to the first floor. There was a well for water. There were frogs in it. We went over to look in the garage, there was a good horse driven carriage made in 1850. Along the border of the land, there were two small abandoned slave houses. The old man who lived there was being forced to leave the house and go to an asylum. While we were trying to get the money together to buy this house, Sterling Winthrop was looking for an assistant to the director of their laboratory in Rensselaer, New York, a change in company. Polly and I did not buy the house.

Sterling Winthrop sent out a questionnaire to thirty different medical schools for the name of who they thought was the best pharmacologist below the age of thirty. My name came up five times and the name of no one else came up more than one time. Perhaps this was the result of standing up in front of 600 people at one of the annual meetings of pharmacologists and criticizing the work of a pharmacologist at the Ely Little Company in Indiana who had been measuring the amount of pain that an individual would have after they swallowed a capsule of Davoron. He had made a mistake in calculating his data and I re-did the calculation in front of the people and pointed out the difference in the results. I just happened to be carrying around the tables in my memory. The initially stated results were thus proved wrong.

Polly and I lived in Albany for three years, and we designed a beautiful house looking out over a valley about three and half miles away from the other houses. It was one of the five houses in a circle and ours was facing south over the valley. It was just the right place. We had a lot of heat from light in the winter time and no sunlight came in during the summer. We had a lovely pool overlooking the little valley. The sun was just right and the shadows were terrific. I was sad when we had to give it up.

Polly wanted to live in Scarsdale, it was an area that attracted people from New York City. The Scarsdale High School was the best in the area and Polly had a brother close by. I wanted to live closer to where I worked. Anyway, we eventually lived in Scarsdale where there was a big hedge about ten feet high in the backyard. I was allergic to it; every time I trimmed the hedge it was like a chemical warfare of sorts. I would stand up there cutting it and wearing a chemical war gas mask. There was no chance of allergy when I was using the mask.

We left the house in Scarsdale after twenty-seven years. The furnace had failed and I had made a temporary repair for it with steel. I thought it wouldn't last more than a year or two. When we sold the house I told them I had fixed it. The people who bought the house hired somebody to examine the fixed furnace, and it worked perfectly. But a year later they had to buy a new furnace.

My Children

Brian's Life

He Stopped Breathing

In 1953, my son, Brian was about four years old when he had come down with a bad case of asthma (croup), which made him have trouble breathing. We had him in the shower, but his breathing wasn't getting any better. Finally he began to get a little blue, so I called the police to take my son Brian and me to the White Plains Hospital Emergency Room. This was known to be a good hospital. There was a foreign resident physician, who was not allowed to do the surgery unless supervised. I said, "He has a very bad croup, and he needs a tracheotomy right now!" I told him to do it. He said, "I'm not allowed to do it." I said, "Then let me have a scalpel. I have done this operation seven times." He said, "You can't have a scalpel, you can't do it." I said, "He is blue, he has stopped breathing!" He said, "You can't do it!" There was a long three foot high by three foot wide platform in front of the resident. I was about to swing up and knock him out and cut Brian's trachea open, just then the Ear, Nose and Throat specialist burst through the hospital entrance door, grabbed the scalpel, and made the incision. Brian started to breathe and his color came back to normal in three minutes. So Brian was all right! He stayed in the hospital for three days and then came home. I had done tracheotomies on seven of my patients and I felt quite competent about doing them. The resident's life had been preserved. The opening of the trachea was about one and a half inches long. It gradually closed without any stitching over a period of about two years.

Brian "Boy Scouts Leader"

We lived for twenty-seven years in Scarsdale, New York. It was a small community. My two sons, John and Brian were in the Boy Scouts. There were four or five Boy Scout groups in Scarsdale. Brian was the leader of one of these groups and each group competed with one another. Brian thought, "What would give the highest reward to all of them?" Brian felt that hiking would give the highest reward. He was thirteen and a half years old. He decided that they were going to make a march during the Spring Break through the Appalachian Mountain trail for sixty-six miles. They would start at Haywood, Virginia on Route 609 near Route 231, which was located close to Culpeper, Virginia. They would go for sixty-six miles and would finish within six days. Their eight months of training would start when school began in September. Five days of the week he called each boy in his patrol and asked if he had done his homework and if he had walked five miles that day. On most Saturdays they marched twenty miles on mountain trails similar to the Appalachian Trail in Shenandoah Valley. He had geodesic copies of the areas in which they would be hiking, so on Saturday's they would practice hiking in areas similar to what they would encounter when it came time to do the march the following April to the Spring Break.

It was a two hour drive to the Appalachian Trail where they would be doing the hiking. When it was time to do the hiking they were in great condition. His older brother John was also going with his group. John was two years older than Brian. Brian had a map for the Appalachian Mountains. Brian's Boy Scout group was going faster than any other group. The other Boy Scout leaders could not have done it! Brian's patrol group had obtained the highest record of any other patrol. Other Boy Scout groups came and marched only four up to seven miles. On Saturdays there were the mountains that were near to Scarsdale. It was a two hour drive. They took sixty-six hours to complete for the march of sixty-six miles.

One of the boys in his group had always been difficult for his parents. He would not do the things he should do for school or the things they asked of him. After he joined Brian's group in the scouts he ceased being difficult and when they were training for this hike. The parents were very happy because their child was behaving very well. He was doing all his homework and everything else; all because he wanted to be one of the boys in the Boy Scout troop who were participating in the hiking. One of the boys who wanted to be in the patrol was overweight, but during the period of training he lost about twelve pounds, due to all this extra exercise. He was down to a good strong athletic figure. At the end of the hike his parents came down to pick him up and take him back to Scarsdale along with some of the other boys besides them. We were driving behind that car and could see the boy's mother was feeding her son and the other scouts lots of cookies. The other scouts in our car behind said, "There goes momma shoving cookies down her son's throat!"

Brian was hard to handle for some of the teachers in school. During his first year at Scarsdale High School, Brian challenged the English teacher on the use of English which caused arguments. When he was a junior, he felt the senior class should try to evaluate the quality of teaching at the high school. The senior class thought that was a great idea. He got the senior class together and asked what they should look at and how to go about it, etc. For all the different subjects someone would collect the records of all the students in that class. Then they would analyze the information and present it to Brian. This was quite a feat for a boy from the junior class to be giving orders on what should be done with the senior class. The principal of the high school heard about it, but he couldn't do anything. It was being done in the homes of the high school students, not in the school. They give the analyses to the Parent Association.

College and Beyond

When it came to going to college, Brian was interviewed by three universities, Harvard, Caltech (California Institute of Technology) and Yale. He was accepted by all three schools. He decided to attend Caltech, probably because it was the farthest from home. He studied at the Department of Biology after graduating. He continued his studies there and obtained his PhD (Doctor of Philosophy) at Caltech and then stayed on to work there. Brian wrote a book with one of the professors at Caltech. When this professor received an offer to go to Harvard he said, "Only if Brian Seed can come to Harvard also." Brian had been working with the professor in the Biology Department at Caltech. He went to Harvard with him and became a professor at Harvard. There was another professor in the biology department at Caltech whom the students did not like and generally would go to Brian if they had any questions. The professor became very annoyed, but there was nothing he could do about it. The professor was upset that none of his graduate students respected him. After two years of teaching at Harvard, Brian became a professor at Harvard.

While Brian was a professor at Harvard, he invented a way of making insulin that increased its viscosity by five fold. One could use a smaller syringe to inject, because now a person with diabetes would only need one fifth the amount of liquid. When it came time to get patent rights, a friend of his had become the dean. He told the dean that if he let his lawyers get the patent rights he would lose two million dollars. Nevertheless, the dean let the lawyer do it, and Brian was right.

Brian is now fifty-two years old. Five years ago he decided he wanted to work on quantum mechanics but he needed to have someone to talk to every week in order to keep his interest up. I volunteered, so I talk to him almost every Sunday evening. The problem he is working on is the discrepancy between the theory of relativity and quantum mechanics. This particular problem has been around for seventy-five years. It is very exciting.

Eight years ago, Brian invented a drug called "Enbrel" which is very useful in treating rheumatoid arthritis. The dean at Harvard Medical School, who was a friend of Brian's before he became dean, let Brian negotiate the patent rights. He negotiated 0.5% of gross sales for himself, the same amount for his laboratory, 1.0% for his department, and 2% for the MGH hospital. Sales are now well over a billion dollars. The lawyers at the MGH hospital have just recently discovered the contract for the patent rights on Enbrel had a clause that says if Brian went to another medical school the money would be go with him to that school. The lawyers have renegotiated the contract so that the money stays at Harvard, much to Brian's amusement.

The director of the Health Department of the Chinese government has asked him to help with China's problem with AIDS. Brian has set up a pharmaceutical company in Shanghai where he is working on inventing new drugs for treating AIDS. The patent rights would then be in China and this would dramatically lower the cost of the medicine to the Chinese people. He is financing it out of his own pocket and has learned to speak Chinese.

Matthew helping his grandfather with the blueberries plants

Elizabeth's Life

My youngest daughter, Elizabeth Karashin, is now fifty years old and is a radiologist in Pittsburgh. She started out in electrical engineering and then switched to medicine. She worked at the University of Pittsburgh and now she is working on her own. She reads x-rays that are sent to her by phone technicians and x-ray laboratories. She completes a full written report based on the x-ray provided and then sends the report to the doctor that ordered the x-ray. The doctor can then review the report and provide the diagnosis for the patient. She has a husband and three children. The youngest, Matthew, is fifteen years old and is in high school. He is very good in mathematics and earns all kinds of awards in competitive math contests. He does well in other topics but is not always at the top. He does not have the same competitive spirit of his uncle Brian. Elizabeth's oldest child, Willie, is twenty-five years old who has a degree in Aeronautic Engineering from Purdue University and is currently working for Lockheed Martin on the design of the F16 Fighter Jet. Elizabeth's second child, Catherine, is twenty-three years old. She graduated from Purdue. She started out in the engineering school in Material Sciences, however after one year she switched to Social Sciences and is working for a Master's Degree in the area of study. While at Purdue as undergraduate she noticed that there were no programs or organizations for women. Catherine founded the Purdue Organization for Women Equality Rights (POWER). It was very successful and was taken over by Purdue University after she left the undergraduate school. She is engaged to marry Justin Conner.

Elizabeth and her husband still live in Pittsburgh. Additionally they have a summer home located in the mountains in West Virginia which is two hours from their home in Pittsburgh. It is a two-acre piece of property that not only contains their custom built home but they also have a lake and a river runs along the edge of the property. Use of the lake and river are their property but the people in a town a mile away tend to use the water without much problems.

Patricia's Life

My oldest child, Patricia Seed, is a full professor of history at University of California-Irvine. She had been lauded for her use of technology in the classroom. She encouraged her students to turn in images and maps as an alternative to written reports. Her research areas have included comparative world navigation and cartography (the art or technique of making maps or charts). She received her bachelor's degree from Fordham University in 1971 and her Master's degree from the University of Texas-Austin in 1975. She then went on to receive her doctorate from the University of Wisconsin-Madison in 1980. Her husband, George Marcus, is Chairman of the Department of Anthropology at University of California-Irvine and is probably one of the top four in that field in the nation, if not the top. They have two children, Rachel and Avery.

Patricia is an accomplished historian. She has published numerous articles and books in different fields and has held several editorial positions. Her books were both awarded prizes for being the best work in that field. She is very gifted at learning foreign languages. She speaks Columbian Spanish and Portuguese equally well. She has a website. The site deals with the history of sailing and all that would encompass the sailing, such as ocean currents, ships and many other topics.

John's Life

My son, John, earned a Ph.D. in Pharmacology from Michigan State University in 1979. His post-doctoral position was at the Johns Hopkins University Bloomberg School of Public Health, where he was promoted after two years to the position of Assistant Professor. He left Johns Hopkins in 1986 to work at the National Cancer Institute. In 1990, he co-founded with his brother Brian, a company that currently manufactures supplies and provides services for the DNA sequencing industry.

John is married and has two boys. His son, Kevin, is twenty-three and is an auto mechanic in Pittsburgh. His son, Randall, is twenty years old and is a sophomore at McDaniel College in Maryland.

Polly Had A Breakdown

When Patricia was ten years old, John Lindon was eight, Brian was six and Elizabeth was four, my wife Polly had a break down. It gradually developed to the point where she could not do anything. One morning she was sitting on the edge of the bed in her night gown. She didn't talk, she didn't respond, she didn't look around, she wasn't moving. I got the children dressed and fed them breakfast. The school was a five minute walk from the house and I sent them off. I called a good friend of mine, Dr. Mickey Stunkard. He was the chairman of the Psychiatry Department at the University of Pennsylvania at that time. I had worked with him during my internship in the Massachusetts General Hospital. When I called him, he stopped his work immediately and came to Scarsdale to see us. He immediately arranged to have Polly taken to the Psychiatry Institution of the University of Cornell, which was near Scarsdale, our home. She stayed there for nine months. I hired a German woman to come to our house and live with us with her six year old son. She taught my children to speak German and stayed with us until Polly could handle it. Polly didn't see anybody until the eighth month when she came home and spent the day. The next Saturday, she came and stayed home for good. All went well and the German woman and her child left.

Polly Improved

From then on Polly improved and became active in the Girl Scouts in Scarsdale. She also became active in a new catholic church that was built two blocks away. She was regional representative for Scarsdale West Winchester Scouts, the total of all the Girl Scout troops in the Winchester Borough. She obtained thirty-six acres of heavy woods for the Girl Scouts. She also had a small building in the woods where the scouts could stay at night, if it got cold.

One very popular thing for the Girl Scouts in Scarsdale was the annual trip to France during the Spring Break. All through the year the girls were busy earning money to make enough money for the cost of going to France. Unfortunately, the trip to France was cancelled because Scarsdale was considered to be a part of Winchester and the people in Winchester were much poorer and their children could not earn enough money for the trip.

At the time of my 50th reunion, the dean was mentioning the names of the members of the other groups that were celebrating their alumni from my class and productive professors some of whom were Harvard professors. Some of my classmates were jealous because none of their children were professors. Brian had become a full professor. I was sitting with the undergraduates. When the wife of one of my classmates yelled out to me from fifteen yards away, "I guess you were right!" She was referring to the time when I stopped dating a girl because she wasn't very bright and I wanted to have bright children. I was right. The woman that I stopped dating had a rough life, including becoming an alcoholic.

Polly's Breast Cancer

After living twenty-seven years in Scarsdale, Polly developed cancer in the breast. Polly was too sick to come to the reunion. Polly and I had an apartment on Witherspoon Street in Princeton, New Jersey. Polly developed heart disease and had to stay in bed. She had three artificial heart valve implants. I stayed with her as much as I could and took care of her for the last four months of her life. She was cared for at home in the apartment, until she died. While she was dying Polly's heart was still beating for another two weeks after her brain was dead. When her heart stopped, I called a nurse to come over to verify the death. She died of heart disease. I made arrangements for her to be buried in the Presbyterian Cemetery in the center of Princeton, at the corner of Wiggins and Witherspoon Streets. I made provisions for myself and for my present wife to also be buried there when we die.

Polly was years older than me and very careful about revealing her age and that she had a degree from Harvard University. She let me know this before we got married, but nobody else knew her age.

Winthrop Laboratories – 1950

Before I joined Winthrop Laboratories in 1950, they had gone to thirty different medical schools across the country asking who they thought was the best of the current young pharmacologists under the age of thirty. My name came up five times, while no other name was mentioned more than one time. As a result, Winthrop hired me.

One of the problems they had at Winthrop was that the chemical that prevented fungal infections on potatoes left bits of white powder on the potatoes. The residue deterred people from buying the potatoes, but if they appeared to just have dirt on them people would still buy them. That was just natural. My job was to make that chemical look just like dirt! To this day, they still use my method of making the chemical for the prevention of mildew and other fungal infections on potatoes. It was simple: put some hard carbon and iron rust; mix them together with the white powder that prevents fungus and then one has something that one could not distinguish from dirt. All of the potatoes ever since have been covered in this "dirt". All the potatoes you buy with a little dust on them are free of mold. One never sees potatoes that have mold on them unless one grows the potatoes in one's own backyard. To have sterile potato skins without the powder, they have to wash them carefully with sterile water and store them in a very dry place. If such a sterile potato were placed in a normal environment, there would be mold growing on it within a week.

Pigs Were Dying

Another problem that came to the attention of Winthrop Laboratories was that pigs were dying in England and nobody knew why. When I heard about their symptoms, I recognized that they were suffering from solanine poison and were probably getting it from green potatoes, since solanine is a poison found in potatoes. I suggested that they boil or bake the potatoes before feeding them to the pigs. They tried it and it worked; the disease disappeared.

Green Potatoes

Eating the skin of a potato can be dangerous if the skin is green. When a potato is dug out of the ground it is a grey, brown color. If allowed to be at room temperature and exposed to sunlight, the skin around the stem will become green. The green color is due to the synthesis of chlorophyll. At the same time the skin will be making some glycoalkaloids, the most common of which are solanine and chaconine. The synthesis of glycoalkaloids is completely independent of the chlorophyll, but the green color is a signal that glycoalkaloid is being made. If one keeps the potato cool and out of the light, the glycoalkaloids will be made in only small amounts. The amount of glycoalkaloid in a potato or the potato skin is not influenced by cooking, frying, boiling, baking or steaming. The potato glycoalkaloids may make inflammatory bowel disease worse. The presence of inflammatory bowel disease is highest in the countries where fried potato consumption is the greatest. The symptoms of glycoalkaloid poisoning are generally the same as those of atropine but they might cause headache, fatigue, nausea, vomiting, abdominal pain and diarrhea. In general, however, it is hard to get enough potato glycoalkaloid to make one sick because I invented a powder that is dusted on the potatoes to prevent the glycoalkaloide from growing.

Epilepsy Treatment

While I was doing research in Winthrop, one of my jobs was to evaluate a new drug for treating epilepsy. I obtained permission to go to New York State Epilepsy Asylum (about sixty miles south of Rochester, New York). About three days before I was scheduled to go there, I spent three hours one evening looking up how to interpret the recordings of an Electroencephalogram (a machine that detects the electric activity of nerves in the brain). When I got to the epilepsy asylum, I asked them if they had equipment for taking Electroencephalograms. They did, but it was an old machine and I had put it back into activity

They had purchased a high quality machine for $4,000 in 1950 which was then a lot of money! They already had it for one year and it did not work and the company's repairman could not repair it. He had tried four times and was unable to get it to work. I asked the director if I could take a look at it. He allowed me; I went in and took it all apart. About two or three hours later the director came to see how I was doing. He saw me sitting cross-legged on the floor with resistors and vacuum tubes scattered around me. He said, "You know, that's a $4,000 machine!" I said, "Yes, I think I can fix it." He said, "Okay," and went on his way. By four o'clock that afternoon I had it working. The director came by and was relieved to see that it worked.

The next morning, the neurologist at the asylum, who had been interpreting electroencephalograms for fifteen to twenty years, asked my opinion on the one he was reading. I said, "Looks to me like it's a lesion (abnormality) in the parietal (part of the brain) area." He said, "That's what I thought." He told the director of my ability to read electroencephalograms, which made a big impression on him. He insisted that I become the Neurological Consultant to the New York State Health Department. He had me appointed as a neurologist for the New York State Health Department. I was very surprised and honored.

In order to keep costs down at the asylum, the New York State Health Department tried to do as many things as possible using their patients. One of these was the tailor shop where clothing could be made, repaired and cleaned. I talked to the man who ran the tailor shop who told me about how he learned to run it. Many of the people who worked there were patients. He noticed that whenever he corrected a man for making a mistake, even in a mild manner, the other workers had seizures. If he did not make any comment about the error there would be no seizures. When a man made an error, he was told to stop what he was doing and was given something else to do. He would show him how to do it, even if he had done it before. Two or three days later, he would ask someone else to do that work that had been damaged and show him again how it should be done.

Helping Control Seizures

One time when I was setting up a fourteen patient ward, the nurses were discussing what sort of equipment and supplies I would need. While a nurse was asking me about thermometers, a patient came up and got involved in the conversation. Suddenly she had a seizure. All the nurse did was put her foot out to catch the patient's head on her foot and didn't take her eyes off me. She kept talking to me. This was the first time I ever saw an epileptic seizure and this patient was down on the floor, shaking away, having a Grand Mal seizure. I couldn't for the life of me, concentrate on what supplies I needed!

Another of the patients was about five and half feet tall and 160 pounds and whenever she had a seizure, she would go "Uhhhhhhhhh," and move towards the nearest person and try to follow them and throttle their neck. The nurses who worked in that ward carried around a loose long towel.. When they would see the patient start to go "Uhhhhhhhhh," they would rush over and flick the towel around her neck until she silently sat down. At this point, they could let the towel loose and it would be all over.

There was a Catholic chaplain at the New York City epileptic seizure asylum. There were about one hundred and sixty Catholics for Sunday afternoon mass. The pews consisted of two seats attached together with pads for kneeling and the nurses could remove patients who were having seizures into a nearby room. These rooms were fully padded and the patients would remain there until the seizure subsided. If the priest's homily was focused on behavior there would be thirty to forty seizures. The priest quickly learned and realized that he had to be careful about what he said.

I Told You Three Years Ago

During my first six months at Sterling Winthrop, I made three suggestions of a compound that might be useful. He didn't accept any of them. One of them was a compound that later on Merck made and another one was later made by IC Garland in Germany. At any rate, all of these companies made the same compound that I spoke of; however I had been told at Sterling Winthrop that they were not interested in them earlier. During my third year with Winthrop, Merck came out with their drug and director told them they had to assign people to that drug project right away. I said to him, "I told you three years ago that the drug would be a good drug and by now Merck has left up all the possibilities and filed for patents on it. There is no point in going ahead and assigning any people to work on anything in that area, Merck has covered it." The director said, "no, no, no." So he assigned five or six people to work in that area, which was a little bit disturbing. Then about two or three months later IC Garland came out with the second recommendation and again, he said to me, "It's very important that we must get people in there." And I said, "No, they have got the patents on it and I'm sure that they have worked all possibilities around that drug and it would not be worthwhile." They still assigned a group of six or seven people to work in that field. About a month or two later the third company came out with my third suggestion and again he assigned people to that. I said to myself, this place is going nowhere; this man is really not very bright. It's going to be a disaster. So, I had quite a difficult time considering if I wanted to stay with the company or not. If I stayed with the company, I was sure I would be the director in the future, but that would be maybe ten or fifteen years down the road. Did I want to work with him for that period of time?

I began to have asthma attacks for the first time in my life. When I left Winthrop the asthma went away. I decided that I was going to quit and I wrote a letter to his bosses in New York City explaining the errors the director was making. I wrote this letter during my last few days of working there. Because I didn't want to go completely behind his back, I showed the director the letter that I had completed, although I did not tell him that I already sent it to his bosses in New York City. He said, "If you send this letter, then you will be fired!" I said, "Yes, that's right." I knew he would fire me because I showed it to him, but I wanted to make sure he knew about it. I really wasn't interested in taking his job. That was on a Friday and by Saturday at noon, I started calling friends in pharmacology letting them know that I was interested in getting a job and that I was no longer with Winthrop. Three days later I had a job with Burroughs-Wellcome, another pharmaceutical company.

For about the next three months, I was riding to Albany on Friday afternoons and staying there with my family until Sunday late evening, and then ride back down to Tuckahoe, New York, where the company was located. I had to take a lot of amphetamine in order to make the long drive and stay awake. I got the effect of too much amphetamine and began hallucinating. I called my friend, Van Aimee, who said, "John you are just taking too much amphetamine, stop it and you will be fine." And he was right.

Burroughs – Wellcome – 1952

At Burroughs-Wellcome, there was a man I was not fond of. Later on, the fellow who I was working with the first time and had suggested he should be in charge of a group in the Army's Chemical Warfare. He suggested to the president that he was being used. He left and brought in another fellow who I also didn't like very well. The differential equation I had put together on how glucose metabolizes in the body with a fifth order non-linear differential equation was difficult. I showed the equation to him and with some disdain he pointed out that he didn't understand things like that. It made him feel like an idiot.

The president at Burroughs-Wellcome had met a physician on the west coast who was getting great results with pseudo-ephedrine for treating eye problems. He was impressed and thought the company should be selling it and it would do very well. I felt that anybody could just take an ephedrine and dilute it down by a factor of thirty. The president of Burroughs-Wellcome said that really didn't matter. They could sell ephedrine in the form of pseudo-ephedrine and it would sell. I couldn't see how that would happen, but it turned out that he was right and I was wrong. I said pseudo-ephedrine is exactly the same as regular Excedrin except that is was $1/30^{th}$ as effective. That was my mistake to point this out. The company's director said it didn't matter it will sell. So Excedrin sold and they made a lot of money, and I absolutely couldn't understand it. A lot of doctors don't realize the pseudo-ephedrine is exactly the same pharmacologically as Excedrin.

I liked to test drugs out for the pharmacologist. If one brought back a report that the drug was not too good, they would question this and that. A chemist treats his drugs the same way a mother treats her newborn child. Even if a report says that a chemical is not wonderful, the chemist assumes that the tester has made a mistake. I had a drug that I thought I wanted to have separated out into isotope components. Isotopes are the various forms in a chemical element, that have the same number of protons in the nucleus (atomic number), but having different numbers of neutrons in the nucleus (the atomic weight). I asked the chemist to do if for me. Three months went by and he hadn't done anything. So I took off time to work on it myself. In just three days (I started on Monday and by Wednesday) I had isolated the isotope. I attached it to a crème of ole? isontoni that would then separate the two chemical compounds. Then they asked me to give them some. I said, "How much do you want?" They answered, "One Gram." So on Thursday morning I gave him a gram. They went ahead and tested it and it was indeed exactly what I had done. From then on, since I had shown them that I could do what they could not accomplish, they no longer questioned anything I did. That was it.

After a few years the current director of the laboratory, who was in that position for a long time, decided he wanted to quit. They were then looking for a new pharmacologist who could do the job. I suggested to them the man who was in charge of the sixteen of us in the army. This man came here to Burroughs-Wellcome and was interested in the position. He felt it was time for him to get out of the army. He was at Burroughs-Wellcome for four years as Director of Pharmacology. For the preceding twenty years, there were two pharmacologists at Burroughs-Wellcome who were turning out very good work. However, they weren't producing very large quantities of anything in particular. The two of them later went on to win the Nobel Prize, which is quite a large event. This was ten years after they left Burroughs-Wellcome. So then, the former army man decided he would like to be financed by the army. He was no longer excited by the work at Burroughs-Wellcome. The company brought in another new man. I didn't get along well with the new man. I impressed him with the work I was doing on computers. So, I left Burroughs-Wellcome and went to take care of the patients at the House of Calvary.

Morphine Study

At the time the Cross-Bronx Expressway was built, one of my patients was a carpenter working on building the expressway. He was a junkie using morphine, shooting up while working on the expressway. I told him, "While you're taking heroin, you really can't think very well." He said, "I have no problem." I replied back, "When there is something that you have never done before, you never can figure out how to do it by yourself. You call some of your friends, **they** look at the situation and then **they** tell you how it should be done. Then **you** carry it out." He looked at me and said, "You are right!" At that time, I had been reading that morphine causes interference with original thinking. Dr. Hood and I were doing a study on the effects of morphine on respiration and I volunteered to take morphine once a week in the study.

At the same time, I was building a computer. Every so often, I took injections on a Thursday morning and ran the tests for respiration for the rest of the day. Some days I'd get my morphine injection and then I would have a hard time figuring out what the next step was. I would usually think about the problem when I was driving home on the nights of the injections. "Oh, that's very simple," I would tell myself. I would come in the next morning, try the solution I thought of during the drive home, and it would work on the computer. I did this twice a week. After the program was finished, I looked back to see when it was that I had trouble figuring out how to build the computer. It always was on the days I had a taken a morphine injection. I never had a bit of trouble building the computer and solving the problems on the other days that I didn't inject morphine.

We realized that the machine could be used for other things, and I started keying in the data to keep records of my supplies. So I wrote a computer program that would always come up with the right answer and everything was properly accounted for. I also figured the Federal Drug Administration (FDA) inventories.

Also at the time, we built a computer with all the steps for anesthesia and it ran perfectly. Only trouble was that it was not very reliable. We had to have four anesthesiologists present when the computer was performing the steps. The computer did all of the anesthesia work during the whole operation without our interference, but it took four times as many people to have the computer do it compared to the single anesthesiologist. We demonstrated that the computer was able to do all the things that needed to be done by an anesthesiologist and we published that.

Silent Competition – Fix It!

Not until my father died did my mother tell me that whenever I accomplished something unusual, my father told her that he could have done that at my age. One of the early examples was the time when I was ten years old. My mother told me to fix the lock on the back door. I protested and said, "I don't know anything about locks! How am I going to fix it?" Mother replied, "Just fix it!" in a stern voice. So I got out a screwdriver to take everything apart, and found out that a spring in the lock was broken. She went out to the hardware store to buy a new spring. I put it in and the lock worked. When my father got home my mother told him that I had fixed the lock and my father said, "I could have done that when I was John's age!" There was no praise ever given to me by my father. It was just something I should do.

Later in high school, I built a desk that I could use at home. In the summer, at age fifteen, I worked as a migrant laborer during the depression. I came back home after the summer with $200. Again, my father said to my mother, "I could have done that!"

Many things happened one after another until I was a professor in Electric Engineering at Princeton University. For the first time ever, my father felt he could not have done that. My mother did not tell me this until after my father had died.

My Father Has Never Listened to Me

After I had been working for Burroughs-Wellcome for about a year, I had sent a letter to a friend of mine, a professor of pharmacology at John Hopkins Medical School in Boston. The letter was part business and part personal. I gave a copy to the President of Burroughs-Wellcome and he sent copies of my letter to eight people in management. He had criticisms of how I used punctuations and language etc. He never told me about it until he had given it to the last person, then he gave it to me. When I received it, I got out the Webster's dictionary and went in to see him and went over all his corrections. I pointed out to him that all the corrections he had made were errors according to the dictionary. He said to me, "If you do this again, you are fired!" I said to him, "You do this again, and I am quitting!" He didn't do it again. Everybody in the company knew he made these grammar mistakes and they didn't want to make a fuss about that again.

House of Calvary

Around 1955, I was doing pain studies for Burroughs-Wellcome at Memorial Sloan Kettering, which is located in the middle of downtown New York City. When I heard about a nursing home for dying cancer patients in the South Bronx called the House of Calvary, I went there to see if it would be a good place to do pain studies. It was a nursing home that was started by a group of Catholic women around 1916. The woman in charge than was Mrs. McParlan, one of the founders who later died at the age of 104. She approved of my wanting to work there because I would be contributing to the effectiveness of analgesics (pain relievers) and I would also be taking care of the patients at the same time. The founder's attitude towards me was that I was there to help the people and that was enough for her.

When I started a pain study, I would ask the assistant taking care of the patient about the patient's disease, how the patient felt, what was bothering them most, what were the problems in taking care of them, etc, while the patient was in the room with us. I used the word assistants because the women who were taking care of the patients were not nurses but by some untrained people who lived in the neighborhood and some religious nuns from the Dominican Order that were dedicated to teaching elementary schools. Taking care of severely sick people was not something that they liked to do, but the need was so desperate that they gave the founder the help. I would then talk to the patient. After the patient had finished, I would then ask them about their pain. If they had pain that would be fit for my study, I would tell them that I had a new medicine for treating pain and if they would be willing to try it. I would give it to them and I would come back every four hours to see how they felt. If it doesn't work by the fourth hour, I would try some other thing. If it was not working and it was after the fourth hour, I would usually give an injection of morphine. The studies were always done double blind. I never knew whether the dose was the test drug or a placebo on any day. At the end of the study I looked at what happened each day. I **did** know that one day it was the drug and the following day it was the placebo. If the pain was getting worse on two successive days the patient was given morphine and was taken out of the study and I continued to take care of the patient.

As time went by, I had more and more patients and more clinical problems that I had never encountered. One day I had a patient with a temperature of 111 degrees Fahrenheit. Standard mercury thermometers in those days did not register anything higher than 108 degrees Fahrenheit. When I saw the temperature indicator was higher than 108, I rushed to the laboratory and took a laboratory mercury thermometer that registered to 212 degrees. I confirmed that her temperature was 111 degrees. We rushed and gave her an ice water enema, two or three times. We brought her rectal temperature to 98.6 and she was alert and comfortable. It was a wild guess. I looked it up afterward and found out that arteries in the colon do not constrict when exposed to cool temperatures. Some twenty years or so later this information turned out to be useful. I was in the hospital and thought I would drop in and say hello to my patient who was there under the care of an urologist. He happened to be there at the same time and was getting ready to leave when the nurse came in and told him that his patient's temperature was 107. I didn't say anything to him, I just shouted out, "Ice water enema". His temperature was down to 98.6 within ten minutes. In ICU units, doctors are frequently trying to cool the patients with covers of one sort or another, but they never use ice water enemas.

The woman who was running the House of Calvary had to go to take care of some financial matters on Wall Street and one of the Dominican Sisters went with her. For the trip she put on her best dress, the one she had when she became a member of the group taking care of the patients in 1916. She was a solidly built woman about 5'10" tall. Her dress had a lot of the frills typical of dresses in 1916. At one point of the trip they were on a subway car and there were no empty seats. In front of them, there was a man smoking, which was not permitted. She took out her hand and knocked the cigarette out of his mouth. He was stunned and frightened. The Wall Street matter was taken care of and they returned with ease to the House of Calvary in the Bronx.

Bats and Submarines

A company had been sold for one hundred million dollars. The money was to be spent for the development of computers for medical services among other things. They contracted me to travel around the country to evaluate the quality of the work being done and to make my recommendations. One of the places I went to was the University of Oregon (60 miles from the ocean), where I met a researcher who was studying bats. He was cutting a Y-shaped hole in the top of a metal disk wire a specific measured depth that he changed for each test. He would decrease the depth of the disk to see how small a depth the bat could detect the depth of the hole. He trained the bats to walk on a wire which was in a "Y" shape. If there was a circular depression in the disk the bat was supposed to walk to one side of the "Y". If there was no hole, he was to go to the other side of the "Y". If the bat was correct, it got a reward of something to eat, a worm, a bug or whatever the bat likes to eat. If he walked out on the wrong side of the "Y" he would not receive any food then.

The research started out with deep holes and they became shallower and shallower. Finally, the hole was $1/10^{th}$ of a millimeter deep, dropped from a yard away from the dropping of the depth and the bat was able to detect it! That was tremendous. It meant that the bat could detect the types of bug, how it fluttered, what its habits were, etc. all from twenty two yards or so away. After seeing the professor's experiments, I decided to give him a good grant. Bats have brilliant detection ability.

When I got back to Princeton, I talked to John Thomas, a professor in Electrical Engineering in Princeton University. Signal Detection Theory was his general field. He gets granted awards of $30,000 per year from the Navy to study on underwater ocean communications; for how to locate submarines and to determine if it was an animal or missile. I put it out to John, "The bats have something going on about sound, etc". I suggested using something similar for the locating of submarines. What the bats do might be useful for detecting submarines.

John Thomas was a guest lecturer in one of my courses. On the final exam, I gave the class the problem of deriving the equation for signal detection theory deriving of an equation. I showed John Thomas the exam and he said, "Hmmmm. I never quite looked at it that way. Let me see if I can do that." He sat down and in about ten minutes he got the answer. I said, "Very good John, you get an A." In the final exam that year, only one student got it right and he deserved it. He was a valedictorian with the highest GPA (grade point average) in his class.

After I was in Oregon, I interviewed a fellow at the Massachusetts of Technology who felt that the way the brain recognizes a straight line was through a Fourier Transform (a type of mathematics). I said to the man, "That's impossible! A Fourier Transform is basically equivalent to doing a second order derivative!" There were two graduate students and a member of the faculty hearing my discussion. "What the brain needs to do is use a 'summer' (an equation that adds things together). With a summer, you have a greater precision of various elements as time goes by. The Fourier Transform just makes it fuzzier." The fellows were shaken by it, because I was right. The Fourier Transform was not the way to go. He had written a book and gained a lot of publicity, but did not get tenure at Massachusetts Institute of Technology!

Nothing is to Happen to Dr. Seed

The first day I worked in the South Bronx, an episode occurred that impressed the heroin dealers in the area. They sent out a word that nothing was to happen to me and nothing did. However, one time, about six years after I had been there, a junkie tried to get into my car and he has never been found.

Everybody in the 42nd Precinct in the Bronx knew who I was. I knew practically everybody in every apartment. I felt very safe in the neighborhood. Little children to grandmothers and great-grandmothers all knew who I was. Grandma sitting on the porch of the apartment during the hot summer days always said hello to me as I walked town the street and everybody knew – "Nothing is to happen to Dr. Seed."

Couldn't Kill a Doctor

One time, two drunks came in. One of the drunks threatened to kill me because I wasn't taking care of his buddy quickly enough. His buddy had to wait because it was somebody else's turn. His buddy wasn't all that sick, but his friend thought I should be more concerned. I closed up the examining room. I locked the three doors in the clinic which where the examining rooms were I was in one of them by myself. He was out in the corridor yellowing, "Tell me which room you are in so I can come in and kill you!" I wasn't about to tell him.

I called the police and nothing happened. I called the police a second time and still nothing happened. Then I came to my senses; the police were not going to bother with this. To them it was so trivial and common. I called up a few patients and said to them, "There is this drunk over here trying to kill me, would you come over and help me out?" In the meantime, the drunk tried to burn the clinic down. He put a cigarette lighter underneath the curtain. The curtain was made of fiberglass, which doesn't burn very well. Finally, my patients arrived and escorted him out of the clinic. As a last way of expressing his anger he took a brick and threw it at the front door, which he thought was glass. The only trouble was, it wasn't glass, it was bulletproof Plexiglas and it just bounced off the door. His day was ruined. He couldn't kill the doctor, couldn't burn down the building and couldn't even break down a glass door. He just couldn't do it.

The next day I wrote him a letter telling him that he wasn't welcome in the clinic and that he should make arrangements to get his medical care elsewhere. A week later he came in sober. I told him, "When you are sober, you are a fine fellow, but when you are drunk, you are very dangerous. We don't have anybody around here who can handle you. Jacoby Hospital (the city hospital) has a policeman on duty all day long to handle this kind of problem. So you will have to go there when you are sick." His mother, father and brother thought I was reasonable with him and he didn't hold anything against me. The neighborhood didn't think I was being unfair to him at all, it worked out very well.

Fake Seizures

In a Grand Mal seizure, the entire body moves, but both sides move synchronously. Wherever the muscles are strongest, that part of the body will shake. It is always symmetrical for Grand Mal seizures. When I was working at the Martin Luther King Health Center, some patients would fake having a seizure in order to get attention and sympathy. They would have one arm going this way and the other arm going another way and so forth. It was obviously a fake seizure. When a fake seizure was recognized, the patient would be picked up and dragged down to the garbage. The patients finally gave up that act.

Barricade Herself

On the first day that we started the clinic, one of the patients was a woman who had trouble with her ex-husband. After taking her history, it was clear that her husband was a paranoid schizophrenic with homicidal tendencies. I told her how she could barricade herself in her apartment with her children and get away from him. She lived in public housing and the walls were steel and concrete. I told her how she could put her chair and table in a certain way that nobody could possibly break in. I said, "Leave your children in the apartment. Come on to see me, but get out here in a way that he won't see you and then walk where he might see you. Go back to your apartment; I will walk a hundred feet or so behind you. When your ex-husband sees you, he will come up to talk to you. When he does that, I will start to talk to him and while I'm talking to him, go home with your children and get out and leave. I will keep on talking with him for a while."

It was a very hot day in July. After intercepting the man and talking to him about a variety of topics, he started to wander off and I went along. I went after him, going in and out of abandoned building for about twenty-five minutes. Annoyed, he started to turn on me, so I decided it was time to leave. A large number of people saw me talking to him, and they knew he was a pretty ugly character. The woman had reached the apartment and off she went with her children. After I left him, he went to the apartment and could not get in, so he got two of his friends and they would hit the door at the same time three times. The next day, they came again and were not successful. They did not come a third time. I did not know where she went and I had no contact with her until ten years later when she came to get her mother who had lived in the neighborhood ever since. Her mother had to move because the house had been burned.

Her daughter took her down to New Port, Virginia with her and her children, where she had a good staple job. She had obtained a job there, and started a program for getting jobs for black women. It was in the newspaper. She ended up with a nice home in the suburbs and a peaceful life.

Man, You Got to Be New Here

On New Year's Day we usually kept the clinic open until 5:00 pm. It was my turn to run the clinic. While returning to my car later that afternoon, I walked past a man who was just outside a bar who said, "Hey white boy, this is a dangerous neighborhood, this is the ghetto, you shouldn't be around here." I said, "Man, you gotta be new here." I walked about fifty feet down the street and I ran into a patient, stopped and chatted with him a little bit, crossed over the street to the other side, ran into somebody else, stopped and chatted with him, went down the street a little bit further. I got to the corner, stopped and chatted with another patient, turned around the corner and I waved to that first black man.

I Ought to Steal Your Car

Word had been passed out by the "hierarchy" that nothing was to happen to me. The drug dealers informed the pushers that nothing was to happen to me and the pushers would then inform the junkies of the same thing. It was 1968 and one junkie was so indiscrete as to try to get into my car and he's never been found! One day I had seen a fight. The fellow who lost seemed down in the dumps about it and as I was walking by he said, "I ought to steal your car." I said. "You'd better not." He said, "What do you mean I'd better not?" I said, "I have friends, I think you'd better not because if my friends don't go before a judge, you would be lucky not to be thrown in jail!"

Heroin Dealer

Mr. X had committed a crime selling heroin. They had the evidence on him and he was to be arraigned on a Wednesday. Anything that could be done to delay that arraignment past Wednesday would mean he would get off with a much smaller penalty. If he was arraigned after his parole was up he would get two to three years in jail. If he was arraigned before his parole was up, he would get about forty years. So he came to me a week before his arraignment and said, "You have to find some way of helping me." At first I couldn't do anything for him. I did a very careful physical examination and found a nodule on one of his vocal chords. So I told him to go tomorrow morning at 8:00 am to Jacoby Hospital, which is the city hospital. I told him, "By 12:30 in the afternoon some nice young resident was going to come around and examine you and find that nodule and will want to admit you to the hospital." So he got there at 8:00 a.m. and by 12:30 p.m. he was examined by a young resident. He complained of the correct symptoms so that the resident would examine his vocal chords and find the polyp. The resident said, "Mr. X you've got to go into the hospital right away. Can you make it on Monday?" Mr. X said, "Well let me see." He takes out his calendar and says, "Yes, I can make it on Monday." So Monday he was admitted to the hospital. Then his lawyer called the judge and told him they were going to operate on Mr. X for cancer of the larynx. So the judge postponed the arraignment for three months. Mr. X was a very good friend of mine, so it worked out very well for him. The resident who put him in the hospital knew nothing about a possible arraignment or anything like that, nor the fact that he was a major figure in the neighborhood.

Mr. X had known me for thirteen years. He told me how he ran his business. He takes a plane to Acapulco, Mexico, rents a car and driving about one hundred and fifty miles north well into Mexico to make his deals. He would carry $50,000 in cash with him, make his deals, and then fly back to the Bronx and wait for the delivery. He did that two or three times a year to get his delivery of heroin. First, before they send it to him, they process it. Then the pushers come in and get their heroin from him and deal it on the street. Pushers are the ones who put it in packs and they buy it in bulk from him and put it into little wax paper packages.

Oh, Sorry Doc!

Another episode in my life: It was 10:00 pm on a Monday night and a junkie had pneumonia. I listened to his chest, gave him antibiotics, and decided he needed to be hospitalized. As I was leaving the building, a woman came running in covered in blood. I opened the front door and there was a man with a knife pointed at me. He said, "Oh, sorry, Doc!" He turned and ran off down the street. This was the 42nd Precinct in the Bronx, which averaged a murder every three days.

Sometimes they would drop a person from the sixth floor down the stairwell. They would then pick up the body and place it along the path that I always took to walk back to where my car was parked. I would see the body and call the police. I'd say, "There's a body down the stairwell at 1746 Basking." They would reply, "Okay, Doc we'll check it out." This happened three or four times. People did not want to deal with the police. It was very dangerous for them. They might have accidentally revealed information that the police could use to find out who was selling drugs and where. As a result they too may be found dropped down the stairs!

Another time, I saw a body underneath some cardboard with a stream of blood leading all the way back to an apartment building about a block away. I called the police and said, "There's a body under cardboard at the corner of Basking and Washington." "OK, Doc, we'll check it out."

One of the toughest problems I had in the 42nd precinct was a sixteen year old black girl who came in asking me to help her study. Her parents wouldn't let her study because they thought she was a snotty little kid trying to make them look bad. They did everything they could to keep her from studying. She wanted to get out of the Bronx, she didn't want to live in poverty and she figured the best way to get out was to get good grades in high school, so she could go to college. Her brothers and sisters and parents did everything they could to keep her from studying, so she asked me if I could help her. I got three elderly black couples to agree to let her study in their apartments. I introduced her to the couples from the three apartments and told her to go to one apartment and the next night to another apartment in a different building and so on in an alternating manner. This way her family couldn't figure out where she was and what she was doing. She just studied at night and she eventually graduated as valedictorian of her class.

She got a full room and board and tuition scholarship to Columbia College and went on to become an advanced nurse. Her family didn't want anything to do with her. It was a disgrace to her family for her to be a valedictorian. Nobody in the family had *ever* done that before.

Another Triumph

Another one of my triumphs: A woman had come in after her husband had beaten her. She wondered what she could do about it. It turned out she had two children. Her husband had been doing time for a murder and he had a twenty-five year sentence. He had fourteen more years to go. He escaped from prison and he was on one of the most wanted lists in the United States as an escapee. Telling the police about it was not a viable option because if the police were notified they would interview him to find out if it is true that he was abusing her or was wanted. They then would go back to the communication house to see if they could collect more information on him and plausible evidence. During their absence, he would be so enraged, that he murdered his wife. Her husband killed at least one person already and if his wife had told the police about his abuse, why he was not going to hesitate to kill her. So what does one do? I was puzzled by what to do for her.

I finally came up about a week later with the answer. I told her to go to Brooklyn and rent an apartment, and not to tell anybody about it. Then make further arrangements with a moving company to come in an unmarked truck and move her furniture on one hour notice, and then buy a bottle of vodka. The next time her husband was to start drinking she should open the bottle of vodka and call the movers. And that's what she did. He passed out. While he was passed out the movers came, took all the furniture, and she left with her kids and when he came to, the house it was empty. If he asked about his wife and children, nobody knew anything. I didn't even tell the police about it. It's the police's job to find his family, not mine. If I report him to the police then I ruin my rapport with the neighborhood. They felt free to come to me for advice on anything; this was a great advantage.

Pushers who sold the heroin on the street every so often thought of mixing the heroin with something or other and before they did, they would come in and ask me if that would be okay if they mix this and this with heroin, even if it would give a better high. One of the things they were thinking of doing was an herb that increases viscosity, and they asked me about that. I told them it goes through the system more slowly but the high will come just as fast and won't last any longer just because it's more viscous. However, I told them that the solution which they were injecting will get their lungs into trouble. Every time they had some new idea about what to do to make the heroin a little bit better, they would come to me and check it out first. If they wanted to put a little antihistamine in it, that would be okay, it won't do any harm.

No, No, No, No!

Two professional car thieves came in asking for dolophine drug. I said "that's methadone". "No, no, no, no. Dolophine, dolophine, that's not methadone!" I got a Physician's Desk Reference (PDR) and showed them dolophine. They asked me if I had some. I told them, "I'll tell you what you can do: go buy some methadone." They said, "What do you mean buy methadone?" I told them, "There's a drug store over there on the corner of Portland and Washington." They said, "But it costs us a dollar a tablet!" to which I responded, "Man, what are you, crazy? You're paying three or four bucks for heroin and you complain about a dollar a tablet for methadone?" They said, "But that's for every *packet* of heroin, or one *tablet* of methadone." I told them, "With the *liquid* methadone you get eight times as much. You take methadone everyday for three days, and you'll break your heroin habit. If you're shooting up thirty-four packs of heroin a day, use thirty-four one-gram packets of methadone. Use $34 dollars of methadone for three days and don't shoot up any heroin for seven days. That will give you a good high." They thanked me, went off to buy the liquid methadone and went on about their business.

Stealing a Porsche in 3 Minutes

These professional thieves took an order for a Porsche, a 1933 black Porsche with a specific kind of tires, since people would pay them a premium for finding a certain type of car and stealing it. They cruised around New York City and if they found one, they'd steal it in less than three minutes, regardless of what kind of locks it had. Their record time was thirty-two seconds. If you left your car unguarded for three minutes, it was gone if they were in the neighborhood! If their need for heroin dropped from thirty-four bags a day to three bags a day, they wouldn't have to steal as many cars to support their habit. They would only have to steal a car every ten days instead of every three days so; I was doing society a service.

Get a Professional

One time somebody locked their keys in their car and asked the police for help. The policeman struggled to get the car open. After five minutes or so he still hadn't been able to get the lock open, so I said, "Get a professional." The policeman glared at me. He didn't appreciate that at all. My "professional" patients could have gotten that door open in less than thirty seconds for sure.

My patients knew all the tricks of the trade. They knew that at very low temperatures you could break the seals on the locks to open the doors; they knew all different types of alarms, where they were located, and where the wires went. They would feel around and detect where the little wires were for the alarms, if hidden or not, disarming it, and away they would go with the car! It didn't matter what kind of an alarm you had on your car. They were professionals!

A Good Burglar

Another patient of mine who was not very bright, and slightly awkward as well, had been arrested for burglary. He received an eight month sentence in jail. I didn't know about his arrest at the time, but he had been seeing me fairly frequently, and all of a sudden he was not around. One day he came back to the clinic. I said, "Bernie, where have you been? I haven't seen you for the last eight or nine months?" He said, "Oh, I've been in jail." I asked, "Where about?" he retorted, ""Riker's Island." I followed up, "What for?" He responded, "Burglary." "Well, welcome back." Poor Bernie! He was a nice fellow but he was a rotten burglar! He just couldn't do anything well. I thought to myself, he'd better give up burglary—it takes more wits to be a good burglar then he had. I told him he has to go to Social Security but I do not think that he did.

One day when I came to the clinic on a Monday morning, someone said "Come quick! Bernie is very sick." I went to Bernie's apartment, and there he was stretched out on the bed face down. I touched his leg and the whole body moved. I said, "Bernie's dead. I'm going to call the police." Not only was he dead, he had rigor mortis, stiffness had set in.

The Diabetic

I had a diabetic patient who refused to take his medicine or do anything about it. He ended up going into a coma and his wife wanted him saved. So, I went over to their house and started an insulin I.V. I went out to the front porch and sat there while the insulin was going in. For the next hour while I was sitting there, fourteen young men stopped by to chat, all of them were taking heroin. One of them went home, had a fix, and came back to join the rest of the group, and so it went. Heroin was common in the area during the 1960s and 1970s.

Another Day, Another Body

While several of my patients were policemen, they never asked me anything about the other patients, and I never mentioned anything about them. Murders were quite common. I remember one time in the spring; the police took a manhole cover off a sewer, and pulled up a body, which had a winter jacket on. I said, "Oh, there's Jose! He was hiding down there all the time. He had an appointment for January 15. He didn't keep it and went down in that hole." The man said, "You know him?" I said, "Sure! He lives on Fulton Avenue, Apartment 2A". Another day, another body.

One day, the second medical director at the Martin Luther King Health Center complained about the patients' charts and how none of the lab work was never entered promptly. The return rate for laboratory work, he claimed, was coming back in three or four days. The majority of the doctors, however, disagreed on the rate of return of the laboratory work, not that the lab work wasn't entered properly in the charts. I did a study and took a hundred patients for whom we had recorded lab work. I recorded the time when the lab work was ordered, when it left the office and the time it came back. I found out that the average length of time was twenty-eight days, not three or four days. I did an exact binomial calculation; the probability that we would receive the lab work back in three days, was something like 6.42×10^{23}.

I presented my study at one of our conferences and he was appalled. I was rubbing it in by getting two decimal points to something that was "10^{23}." It didn't make much difference. Ten to the minus twenty-third is an extremely small number. He agreed that my study was a valid statistical study and that he was wrong.

About a year or so later, he was asking for a job with the public health service and came in to talk to me before he left. He asked me what I thought his weaknesses and strengths were. He said, "You're the only person I know whose judgment I trust." So I told him honestly, and he thanked me.

The "1199" Strike - 1976

Hospital workers at Martin Luther King (MLK) hospital went on strike for increased wages. Secretaries were members of the union. The doctors doing their residency at MLK at the time were all communists. When a fellow was applying for a position there, they would question where he voted, did he go to the communist meetings and so on. They never asked questions about the medical competence, just about political beliefs.

The strike was on. They set up picket lines right around the satellite clinic where I was working.

Secretaries, janitors and even some health workers were all members of the 1199 Union, who called a strike. Family practice doctors, who were communists, decided to strike along with the union. I kept my satellite office site open with my wife Polly, who was working with me. The communist doctors felt that patients shouldn't be able to see a doctor at all, so they formed a picket line to prevent patients from coming in to see me in the clinic.

The day before they set up the picket line, a diabetic woman came into the clinic with her eighteen year old daughter who had an abscess. The abscess wasn't quite ready to be lanced so I told her to go back home, put hot soaks on it and come in the next morning. The next day the picketing doctors turned her away. They told her she would have to go to the Lincoln hospital, a city hospital. She knew about what Lincoln Hospital was all about, so she went to the Montessori Emergency room, which was still open. Montessori was a general private hospital two miles north of the office I was working in. She went in, got the abscess lanced, and was told to go back to her family physician (which I was) the next day. Instead of coming with her eighteen year old daughter alone this time, she came in with her twenty-two year old son, who had just gotten out of Riker's Island prison two weeks earlier. He came up to the picket line with a fourteen inch knife with a wide, sharp blade strapped to his thigh, and said to the doctors, "We're going in to see Dr. Seed." The picket line opened wide and he, his mother, and the daughter walked in to see me. I took care of her diabetes and sent her home.

Retinas

I had eight patients who had strange, very unusual retinas. The communist doctors I was working with were not very able and could not see what I was talking about. I asked them what they saw in the back of their eyes and to describe it to me. They said "you see all these strange things when you look in there." I looked in their eyes and what was in the back of their eye was not normal. I sent them off to have a specialist take a look. The specialist found that they all had these rare veins with deformities that were in their eyes. The thing that bothered me the most was that they didn't want to learn about their condition. Eight of them and not one of them wanted to learn.

I brought the communist doctors to see patients who had unusual eye findings in an attempt to teach them. The other doctors examined the retina and couldn't see what the problem was. I recognized it as something abnormal and I sent the patient off to a specialist. They weren't interested in learning how to recognize what a normal retina was like. Those are the kind of people that were going into family practice in those days. They were intellectually retarded.

Nothing To Do With Those Doctors

About an hour later, along came a seventy year-old Puerto-Rican Spanish speaking woman. She did not know English, she had never used public transportation and they told her she could not see the doctor. She had to go to the Lincoln hospital and they told her how to get there, but she knew nothing about bus travel. She went home and cried all night. She came in the following morning at around 8:00 am, the same time that I was arriving at work. The picketers did not get there until 9:00 am, so I was able to see her, take care of her; I made the diagnosis of asthma and began her treatment. I felt very enraged by the fact that a person would have to enlist his/her twenty-two year old son in order to get in to see the doctor. When you're old, frail, or weak, then you can't see him.

I would have nothing to do with those doctors. They threatened to slash my tires; they took the metal uprights on the windows in the front and smashed beer cans against them. They piled pieces of concrete, asphalt, chunks of wood, paper and cardboard against the door. I had to call the police to come take it away. Finally, the strike got settled and Montessori hospital fired all of them. But national labor had hearings on the whole incident and insisted that they each be reinstated. I felt that was unfair and they should have another hearing before the national labor board. The doctors intimidated all the people who were going to present data on my side as to what they had been doing.

The national board told the judge not to admit the evidence on intimidation of witnesses which we presented. Montessori hospital had to rehire the doctors. They operated in the same clinic I did, but I no longer spoke to them. If they had something to tell me about a patient, they had to put it in writing. I would return the response in writing. If I passed them down the corridor, I'd look straight ahead, not acknowledging their presence. That has continued to this day. Since then I have occasionally seen several of these doctors at medical meetings.

Cleaning Pots

I got a letter of recommendation from the Montessori hospital for my skill because I had pitched in and helped during the strike. I did everything I could to break the strike but I would have to say, I have no use for those people. There were times when I wasn't seeing patients; I went up to Montessori hospital to help out with the manual labor. I got cleaner pots and pans to the cooks and got it to them on time. The cooks appreciated how the pots were. At supper time everybody in the hospital had normal meals, I always had steak. The pots that I cleaned were cleaner than what the regular workers did; that's what the cooks said to me. The cooks were in a different union than the ones who were on strike.

You Don't Know Your Ass From Your Elbow

About five or ten years later at Martin Luther King Hospital, a medical director criticized my judgment in handling patients. My stomach turned for about three days and I finally decided I had enough of that. I went in his office and started out by saying, "When it comes to medicine you don't know your ass from your elbow." Then, after that I proceeded to chew him out in about ten different areas where I thought he was incompetent and had poor judgment, so I left. He had two choices, he could just take it and forget about it or he could fire me. However, if he fired me, I was by far and away the best doctor he had in a staff of ten and I had friends in that area of the South Bronx where they sometimes settle problems by killing somebody.

He Didn't Fire Me

If he fired me, he stood about a ten percent chance of getting killed. Did he really want to fire me and risk getting killed? Or was he just going to accept it? He decided the best thing was to forget about it. Since I was twice as productive in seeing patients as the next busiest physician, he would have been really hard pressed since firing would have hurt the hospital and have gotten him in trouble.

Sometimes You Win, Sometimes You Lose

One patient was an alcoholic with a tendency to barge in. He tried to be seen before it was his turn. I never let him get away with it. I'd say, "Go back and wait your turn, I'll see you then. I won't see you any sooner." One day, he was slightly drunk. He said, "I hate you. I'm going to cut out your eyes one of these days." I said, "I'm not afraid of you. You'd have to sober up before you can cut out my eyes and you're never going to sober up, I'm perfectly safe." Another time, he came in and said, "I like you, but I don't know why." For some strange reason, he stopped drinking, got a job, and left the community. Sometimes you win, sometimes you lose.

Morrisania Hospital - 1966

After I left the Martin Luther King Hospital, I went to work at Morrisania Hospital, which had long since been changed to a minor hospital that was open 24 hours a day. I was covering through the night and I had one of the scariest times in my life as a staff member. I was in the emergency room on a hot August night; everybody else had already gone home for the evening. I was sitting at a table and a man came in and he said, "I feel like killing somebody." I said, "Have you ever killed anybody?" He said, "Yeah." I asked, "What happened?" He said, "They sent me to Dannemora." Dannemora was a prison for the criminally insane in New York State. So, here's this fellow at one o'clock in the morning and nobody else is around and I kept talking to him about his background, what he does, what he likes to do and so on. I kept looking around, hoping that somebody would show up. Finally, he got bored. He got up, left the table and walked out into the darkness. As soon as he was out of sight I called the police and gave them a description of the man. He needed to be picked up before he started killing. He had already done it once; obviously he was schizophrenic. This fellow could have smashed me without any trouble. The police never found him.

The Cornea Split Apart

A woman came in and her eye itself had split right down the middle. The pressure in her eye built up so that finally the cornea had split apart. I called up Morrisania Hospital and got a chief resident of ophthalmology there and gave him the description. He said, "I've never heard of anything like that." I said, "I don't care whether you've heard of it or not, do you want to see her?" He said, "Oh yes, send her over here right away!"

Bus Accident

One day, a large truck smashed into a crowded bus on the Cross Bronx Expressway around 6:00 pm. There were fifty-two people on the bus. Morrisania Hospital was two blocks away and all the people were brought there. When the victims arrived, a few were already dead. Three or four were close to death. Four or five looked like they could live for another two or three hours. I was in charge of the emergency room at that time. I stood in the middle of all the activity and commotion with my thumbs in my belt giving orders. A nurse said, "Damn, this is the first time I ever saw anybody standing like that in a crisis like this". I did not do anything else other than stand there and give out orders. My job was not to run around doing things but to see that things were done correctly. I had to call all the surgeons and get them here as fast as possible and also get all the operating room people here quickly. I also called all the nearest hospitals to see how many people they would be able to take care of. I had to get somebody to get the elevator down to this floor and keep it there until two people came to be sent up to the third floor. The elevator was cranky and was sometimes hard to get. The third floor was where the operating rooms were located. Then I started to say who was to be sent where and what treatments needed to be done if they weren't already receiving them. Then I started treating patients myself. One of them was a black man who was a senator in the New York State Senate. He was wearing a very fine, expensive, brown, felt jacket. He had a fracture of his humerus. He said, "It hurts". I said, "I am trying to get your jacket off". He said, "Cut it off". I said, "But that is an expensive jacket". He said, "Cut it off". So I cut it off, put on a splint, and sent him to another hospital. An hour and half after the accident, every thing was taken care of and we were ready for another accident.

Tackled and Handcuffed

A policeman had been shot in the arm and I was stitching up his wound. There were seven policemen in the emergency room when a woman came in. Her face was slashed from one side of her ear to one side of her lip. I was about to sew it up when her husband lunged at me to prevent me from sewing up her face, which was not very wise to do in front of the police. I had just finished sewing up the police officer, and when he came over to interfere with my work on his wife, he was tackled and was handcuffed by one of the other policemen before he hit the floor.

Other Stories from the South Bronx

One time, a poor lady had a fire in her building but her individual apartment never caught fire and water was still running. The welfare department still deemed it "adequate housing" and there was only one apartment in the building that was left out of about thirty. This one was even partly burned, but the old lady's apartment was pretty well intact and the fire did not badly damage it. However, she was then left all alone in an abandoned building with only cold running water. What was she going to do? The natural thing to do was to burn down her apartment so the welfare department would give her somewhere more desirable to live. The expected fire occurred and her apartment was destroyed. I don't know who burned it down. She may have had a friend of hers do it. When her apartment burned down, she got new furniture as well. The welfare department paid for the new furniture and hot running water.

A Desirable Building in South Bronx
(Getting a Good Place to Live)

A group of healthcare administrators and nurses at Martin Luther King Health Center decided to try to renovate four abandoned buildings in the South Bronx. They took the people who were living in the building and organized them. All the people on each floor elected a floor captain. The five floor captains and the building superintendent formed a building committee. The building committee was told what the income would be from rents and what it costs for oil to heat the place. The tenants wanted locks on the front doors repaired, they wanted windows repaired, and they wanted rooms painted. The building committee made those decisions. The committee went back to where prospective tenants used to live to inquire about them with their former neighbors. Were any of the children into drugs? Did they ever have an arrest? If they had a clean ticket then they got permission to move into this building after nine months. These buildings became the most desirable places to live in the South Bronx.

The problem that the New York government has never faced up to is that one can't place irresponsible people in normal housing. There was no discrimination, but prospective tenants were accepted only if they were responsible law abiding people. If anybody was into prostitution or selling drugs or using drugs or anything like that, they didn't get in. The city needed to build housing for the irresponsible people. That housing would have to have reinforced concrete steel steps in the front of the apartment building so that anybody walking up the steps can been seen from the street. They would also be lit by streetlights as well as local lights. There would be no elevators. Windows would have bars on them. Trash and garbage could not be thrown out the window. The toilets would just be a hole in the floor that one couldn't flush. It would be impossible to break the toilet and the sink. The heat would be in the walls so only the manager could change the temperature settings for the heat. It would be under control by the superintendent of the building and it was locked. If anybody in the family was into drugs or into prostitution or any of those kinds of things, the whole family, as a unit, would go out of the safety housing. If they are in safety housing, and they go six months without anybody getting into trouble, they could apply to get back into normal housing. But nobody wanted to hear about that. I wrote it up in the '70's for the "New York Times". They turned it down. Someone someday will wake up to the fact that you can't house irresponsible people in normal housing because they may destroy it.

"Are You Sure?"

Generally speaking, I could put up with all patients, but one time I had a woman who every time I told her anything she'd say, "Are you sure? Are you sure?" Finally, I was so tired of hearing "Are you sure?" and going through a long explanation, I decided she could not come to the office any more, and <u>I was sure</u>!

Roach

Two years before I began working at the Martin Luther King Health Center, I was working in the emergency room of the Morrisania Hospital which was a city hospital two blocks south of the Cross Bronx Expressway. Although it was a city hospital, Montefiore Hospital, which was two miles north, ran the emergency room for Morrisania Hospital. There were large doors at one side of the emergency room where ambulances came to unload patients. In the summer time these doors were usually left open during the afternoon and evening. It was not unusual to hear a voice from more than a block away screaming. There was one incident in which a patient came screaming, "There's a roach in my ear, there's a roach in my ear! Get it out! Get it out! I can't stand it!" The ear canal is ¾ of an inch long and 3/16 of an inch wide. It has been designed to hear tones, not to host roaches. The roach could not turn around in the ear canal so it had to back out. When the patient arrived, I was ready. I put a drop of an antiseptic, Zeferan, which is no longer available, into the ear. Roaches hate the taste of Zeferan and they backed out. My right hand was on the left ear lobe, where the roach was; my hand was flat and perpendicular to the ear lobe with middle of my hand at the opening of the ear canal. When the roach appeared I swept it off within a second and stepped on it within a fraction of a second. I then looked to see if there had been any damage to the ear drum. That roach will never lay eggs in a human ear canal. Some doctors put oil in the ear canal to kill the roach. In five to ten minutes the roach would be dead, and they had to get the roach out with tweezers. Usually it is dragged out in pieces and caution has to be taken not to damage the ear drum. My way is more efficient than the oil technique; I make the roach do the work and climb out.

Later on, when I was in Princeton I had a patient come to my office complaining that she had wax in her ear. She had been in the Emergency Room and the doctor there told her to see her family doctor, and let him irrigate it out. So she came to see me, and I ran water into her ear. Ordinarily, when there is wax in the ear, the water comes out yellow, but this time the water had no color. As the water came out it had six legs and an antennae. It was a roach, and that told me that the patient was likely an alcoholic, because there is no way a roach could crawl into her ear without her being aware of it, unless she was anesthetized. I asked her if she was an alcoholic, and she acknowledged it. She was so embarrassed, she never came back to see me.

Tampons

One day, a woman came to see me because she had an unpleasant odor from her genitals. With a woman aid present, I had her lie down on the examining table with her feet up in the stirrups. I pulled out a tampon which she forgot she put in five months earlier. She was very embarrassed. I took the tampon to another waste basket in a separate, unused room. The patient was extremely embarrassed.

A Difficult Problem

A sixty year old woman, who was schizophrenic and unable to take care of herself, was being cared for by her daughter who was of low intelligence. Both were on welfare. A court order said that they had to take care of their partially blind brother who could barely take care of himself. There was a man who ran a delicatessen on the corner of the street where they lived. He collected their checks and gave them all their meals, paid all their rent and paid for any other things they needed. I tried to get them put into some institution, but was unsuccessful. Time went on and nothing happened that would make it necessary that they be sent somewhere. After three years, the toilet in their apartment became blocked. They never asked for help. However they put urine and stools into the bath tub. When that filled up they threw it out the window. The owner of the building couldn't do anything. They did not know what to do. Who was going to clean the toilets? The owner could have refused to renew the license, but he would have to wait two years before he could force them out. The Health Department informed him that this was a health hazard. The people who lived there certainly did not like it; it was dangerous to enter the building because one might get hit. Finally a solution to the problem came. One of our clinic staff, who was out in the neighborhood providing visiting-care to patients who could not get to the clinic, came back with news that the residents of that apartment had built a small fire on the wooden floors in the living room of that building to keep warm. It was the afternoon in the middle of November and I called the police and asked them to send over an officer who could testify as to what was going on! I was on the scene when they came. There were two sergeants and one captain. I was taking their names and their badge numbers. The captain said: "I've been an officer for thirty years and I've never seen anything like this." I said "I don't care about that. What is your name and badge number, captain?" We took the three tenants over to the hospital, told the story and gave the names and badge numbers of the officers. They were taken without any protest. Lighting a fire on a wooden floor in an apartment building is a major threat to society.

Man Dying

Two fellows brought in a friend of theirs who was blue and motionless. They thought he was dead. When they brought him into the clinic, I reached down and felt a pulse. I had some esthetic narcotics and injected it into his vein and thirteen seconds later he was wide awake. His buddies were in the waiting room, cursing and swearing and I reprimanded them for their actions. I told them, "You behave yourself when you are in here and now go talk to your friend." They went over to their friend and saw that he was in a normal condition and they were very humble when they walked out the door. We kept him overnight because sometimes the effects can wear off. He was fine and he went home the next day at noon time.

Cop Shoots Rat

In the 42nd precinct in New York City almost all the apartment buildings were infested with rats. If the people in the apartments complained to the Sanitary Department of the infestation, the Department was supposed to talk to the owner of the building to make sure the rats were killed. However, the people who were supposed to do the job stated that they inspected the building and found that there was no evidence that the building was infested with rats. The owner of the building paid them off in return for lying about the rats.

One evening a large, sick, and confused rat was wandering around a woman's living room. She was terrified and unable to get the rat to leave the room, so she called the police and asked for help. A policeman came at about 11 and he shot the rat with his 35 mm revolver. When I heard about this early in the morning, I dropped everything and had a young lawyer come with me to see how he might help start an organized program. I picked up some light weight gloves and asked the lawyer to take a pen and pad to go with me to the apartment where the rat had been shot. The building in which this happened had been examined four days before this episode and it was found to be "free" of rats. The woman let us in and I searched three rooms in the apartment and all of them had two or three holes, per room, between the walls and the floors, just large enough for a rat to come through. I put my gloves on and searched the holes to feel how soft the rat droppings were. If they were soft, then they were recent. The lawyer took notes of all the observations. We interviewed the policeman who shot the rat. I also called the "Daily News" and sent them the lawyer's notes, and the next day the front page headline was "Cop Shoots Rat". The mayor of the city was on the hot seat. The director of the Sanitary Department was fired and some lower positions were altered. Every so often something constructive can happen and it happened then.

Burnt Out

If the water in a bathtub ran over, it would cause $1,000 worth of damage to the walls in the apartments below them, but the offender couldn't afford that much. The welfare department was not willing to pay for it to get fixed. If the landlord fixes it, the tenant will do it again and the landlord will give up and not make any repairs. The landlord didn't care as long as the boiler worked and he collected the rental money. When the boiler failed, they abandoned the building and then there's no more heat. The landlord would not make any attempt to get the boiler fixed. The people who live in the building can not make repairs. When the tenants leave a fire occurs in the building. Nobody would know how it happened but a fire would destroy the apartment building and the tenants' homes would be burned out! They could then insist on a heated apartment. The welfare department had never been able to find out how to manage this problem.

Leprosy

A thirty five year old woman from the Dominican Republic used to be in great health and suddenly started feeling terrible. While doing a physical exam, I noticed a hard spot on her forearm, a little bump. It was a leprosy nodule which grows in the nose for four years and then goes into the bloodstream. It is often found in the earlobes because it prefers a cool environment. I called the health department in Atlanta and asked, "Where do I send somebody that has leprosy?" They said, "You have two choices Cargo, Louisiana or U.S. Marine Hospital in Staten Island." Cargo was shut down about a year ago and now everything is left to the Dermatology Clinic at Staten Island. So I sent her there. She had a polyp, it looked like an ordinary polyp, removed from her nose a year earlier at Manhattan Ear and Nose and Throat Hospital. In those days Dapsone, a chemical drug, didn't cure leprosy, but it inhibited growths and prevented her from infecting other people.

415 Pound Woman

A woman who weighed 415 pounds had a very prestigious position in society. On the days when the Welfare/Medicaid checks were given out at the bank, everybody waited in front of her apartment building to go to the bank with her. She would wait until everybody got their checks cashed and then they would all walk home together. Otherwise little boys from the community would run in and hit them hard and knock them down to grab the money from under their bras. But with a 400 plus pound woman by your side, this was no problem. So when the little boys saw a group coming, they decided to wait until they saw a single woman coming out and knock her over and grab the money. Everybody wanted to be the 415 pound woman's friend, and spoke kindly about her.

Man Kills His Daughter

A schizophrenic man felt that his eleven year old daughter was trying to kill him. He and his daughter were under the care of the New York City welfare department. When I heard this, I wrote a letter to the welfare department telling them that it was very dangerous because he might kill his daughter. Nothing was done for three months, so I wrote a second letter. Again nothing was done. Three weeks later, he killed his daughter; I was enraged. I had copies of the letters and told the "Daily News" about it and sent them copies of my letters. They investigated and put the information on the front page. The city was outraged. The Mayor was reprimanded for not being aware of how the welfare department was operated, and there was a talk of having him removed.

A year later, a similar episode occurred. A woman thought her six year old daughter was trying to kill her. As soon as I heard that, I wrote a note to the welfare department telling them that the mother might kill her daughter. It was a hot July day on a Friday around 3:30 p.m.; I decided to tell the local welfare department about it so that they could be thinking about what needed to be done on Monday. By chance, the local supervisor answered the call. I read the letter to her and she said "Oh, my, it is Friday afternoon." In a discouraged voice, she said "Oh, right I won't be getting the letter until Monday morning." Half an hour later, she had a court order to the police that they should take the child from that apartment. A policeman came to the house and told the mother that she was wanted at the police station that was about a block away. The policeman walked with her to the station. She went without telling anyone to take care of her children. He assured her that she would be back in half an hour. As soon as she was out of sight, the police came in, scooped out the children and took them to the hospital. From there the welfare department placed them somewhere else. The police knew the mother because of the number of times she was fighting other people who lived in that apartment. I knew of one episode in which she was welding a two foot long piece of pipe.

(OB-GYN: Error) Fetus Removed

One day I saw a patient who I thought had a problem with an ectopic pregnancy. I sent her to the obstetrical gynecologist and she thought that the patient did not have a fetus in her fallopian tube. The ob-gyn recognized that the risk of both dying was very high. Three days later she came into the clinic hemorrhaging. The patient was rushed to the hospital immediately and the baby was delivered. The baby died, the mother survived.

He Forgot!

The combination of Rivastigmine and Donepezil will cause defecation from nicotine in cigarette smoke. A sixty-three year old man had been taking 1.5 mg Rivastigmine twice a day and five milligrams of Donepezil one a day, for two weeks. When a friend offered him a cigarette, he forgot about the side effects, and took two puffs of the cigarette, and lo and behold, said " Oh, my gosh, I forgot, and the toilet is on the third floor!" he ran up the stairs as fast as he could and got there just in the nick of time. He never smoked again.

He is Dead

I received an aggressive letter from the state attorney in charge of a murder trial. He demanded that I be in his office at a certain date and time. I obliged; upon arrival, I sat opposite him at a table.

Attorney: "Where were you on August 8th?"

Me: "I don't know"

Attorney: "Do you work for Morrisania Hospital?"

Me: "Yes"

Attorney: "What do you do?"

Me: "I'm a doctor in the Emergency Room"

Attorney: "What days do you work?"

Me: "Any day"

Attorney: "Do you ever work on Sunday?"

Me: "Yes"

Attorney: "Did you ever work at Morrisania on a Sunday?"

Me: "Yes"

Attorney: "Did you work on a Sunday in August?"

Me: "I might have"

He pulled out a copy of the Morrisania Hospital Emergency Room sheet for August 8 and my writing showed: "Dead".

Me: "If I said dead, he's dead"

Attorney: "I was just testing you to see if you could be confused by the opposition when this comes to court.

Spirits

In 1966, I was working at the Martin Luther King Health Center, located in the 42nd precinct of New York City half a mile above the Yankee Baseball stadium. Twelve percent of the Puerto Rican people living at the center were schizophrenic. The reason for the high percentage of Puerto Ricans in the 42nd precinct is that if one is schizophrenic one has trouble dealing with other people, so one doesn't earn much money. For example, one of my patients had a job as a file clerk in a large company. She was the fastest of all the twelve clerks and never made mistakes. So they made her the supervisor of all the clerks. Six months later, they fired her because all the other clerks were upset. Since then she was poor, could not find work and had to be on welfare. It would have been better if they had set her back to being a clerk.

Being a spiritualist is inherited. If the patient accepts the diagnosis, the spiritualist will offer to train that person to embrace their new identity, but in exchange must promise never to take medication to treat schizophrenia. The trainee must memorize all the different prescriptions because if treated the person will lose all their "spiritualistic" abilities.

If a patient is schizophrenic, I asked if they have seen a spiritualist. If the answer is yes, I ask them if the diagnosis was "cadena". If the answer is "yes" I would say "That is a mistake, the diagnosis is a name and you should take this medicine." I began to trick them into accepting the forbidden prescription medications. Afterwards, I would prescribe a medication for depression or anxiety that is not on the taboo list. If the first prescription didn't work, I would give them another prescription. As months pass, I would switch over to drugs that are used to treat schizophrenia, since by that time the patient would have confidence in me.

Princeton

In 1979, it was apparent that I could no longer work in the South Bronx. When there once were more than 6,000 people, in 1979 there were only 600; not enough patients to support my family. Although our family lived in Scarsdale, I felt I did not know enough people to start a successful practice, despite my family's involvement with community activities.

Teaching

I decided to go to Princeton and teach Electrical Engineering. I had a well established reputation. I started looking around for an office within walking distance of the hospital and the Engineering school. I heard that they were going to put up a four story building at the corner of Witherspoon and Spring Street. I talked to the people who were planning the building on the corner. They gave me the plans for the building and I gave them advice about what I would like. They made it the way I wanted.

The entrance to the office was by either a ramp or six steps. On the right side of the waiting room there was a large lavatory. There were three examining rooms on the right side and a large one directly at the end. The rent was $4,000.00 a month.

In Princeton, they had been telling me that Witherspoon Street was dangerous and that I shouldn't be walking up and down late at night. I have been walking up and down Witherspoon for twenty years and they have yet to find a body there. It can't be that dangerous!

During my second year, after arriving at Princeton, a group of doctors, of whom I was the leader, wanted to set up an HMO for dealing with insurance companies. There was quite a bit of discussion. Two fellows, another man and I, were for the HMO and another group was against it. To settle the issue, we decided to have a vote. One of the opposing doctors threatened to have my tires slashed and car windows broken. I said to myself, "He doesn't know who I am, if anything happens to my car, I will have somebody from the South Bronx have a little talk with him." Fortunately for him, he didn't do the damage to my car.

Medical School Reunion

I went to my fiftieth medical school reunion. Polly was unable to join me because her breast cancer was too advanced, leaving her too weak. The alumni and their wives were assembled under the tents on the quadrangle while the Dean of the Medical School explained what was being done at the school. He mentioned that Brian Seed, son of John Seed of the class of 1945, was among the thirty seven new professors. I was thrilled that all of my classmates heard that I had a son who was on the faculty!

That evening, a meal was served for the class members and their spouses. As I was approaching the dining table to sit with a couple who I had gone on group dates with fifty one years earlier, I heard a loud voice call to me from about fifteen feet away. A woman said, "I guess you were right," rather than the traditional "Hello John". She was talking about being my ex-girlfriend. I had stopped seeing her after four dates, because I realized she wasn't very bright, and I wanted to have bright children! And I did do that!

Some of my classmates were jealous because none of their children were full professors. In discussing our current careers, none of my former classmates, with the exception of my old roommates and that couple congratulated me. Only a few even made a comment at all. Many of them and their family members were in important medical positions, but none as prestigious as my Harvard and army legacy. Harvard can be a very competitive environment and I enjoyed being at the top.

Polly enjoyed hearing me retell the events of the reunion, especially hearing of Brian's appointment. It boosted her up before she started down to the end. Two years later, she died from the cancer. During that time, Doreen Babbot was her doctor, but not much could be done; Polly paid only two or three visits to Doreen. Polly stayed at home and there was day time help. I cooked supper, ate with her, and cared for her until the help came in the morning. Along with the cancer, Polly also had a number of cardiac and blood pressure problems including an implanted cardiac heart beater. I slept at her bedside for the two weeks until her brain died and then also for the following two weeks until her heart stopped beating. She was buried at the cemetery in Princeton. For the next three years, I kept the grass over her grave green and well trimmed. Some day, I will be buried next to her.

Princeton Church

Twenty years later, when I lived in Princeton, I would sometime tease the pastor Reverend Evasiof Demarcellis, who knew about the seizures at the epileptic asylum by saying to him "Father I have been coming to mass here for ten years and I have never seen a seizure. Your homily is not getting through to them". I had the privilege of giving him a service at the end of his life. He was in the Princeton hospital with severe pulmonary cancer. On a Saturday afternoon when he was close to dying, he wanted to leave the hospital to go to the church rectory where he hoped to pass away. His regular doctor was out of town for that weekend and the nurses felt uncomfortable about putting in an order for him to be sent home. I happened to be in the hospital to see one of my former patients, and decided to pay him a visit. When I saw what was happening I took over the responsibility for his care by writing the order for him to be sent to his church rectory. His regular doctor was mildly annoyed by my doing it. The following day, Sunday, he died with twelve of his friends at his bedside at the church rectory!

One time, during Mass a patient had a heart attack. The priest signaled to me. I made the diagnosis, had him lay down on a pew, and called for the ambulance. They took him away in ten minutes. The Mass continued, but this was only a small activity. After Mass was finished I went to the hospital. It appeared he would survive. That suited me for a substitute for seizures.

However, one time we did have a seizure at mass. A group of people who were patients on tour, who had seizures frequently, were visiting Princeton for a few days. On Sunday, they decided to attend mass at St. Paul. The person in the first row on the first position on the left side of the main aisle had a seizure. The people around her knew just what to do, so it was only a small event.

Tuberculin Testing

I taught statistics at Cornell for about three years during which I made some friends among the students at Cornell who came to South Bronx to help me conduct a tuberculosis study. I wanted to see how much tuberculosis was in the surrounding community using the skin PPD injection (purified protein derivative). An injection was done under the skin to see if a reaction occurred. If a red spot on the skin appeared, this would indicate tuberculosis had occurred, sometime in the past. I told them where to park their car when they came up and how to chain the hood of the car down. As I went out to meet them, I told the people along the street that these are some students from Cornell who have come up to help me and that this was their car. And they say, "Oh, that's nice doc." And then their car was quite safe.

About a year later a new doctor came to work in the clinic. He arrived at 9:00 a.m. and parked his car on the other side of the street. Around 9:30 a.m. one of the employees from the office had looked out the window on the second floor and saw his car was on concrete blocks, the battery missing and the tires gone. The administrator rushed downstairs, and said, "No, no, no, no, no, no, he works here." "Oh, we're sorry!" they said, and put the car back together. That was one hour after he got to work.

We went to the clubs which used to be the commercial stores along the street. This was where heroin users "shot it up". In one, there were about thirteen people. Twelve of them had no problem getting the PPD (Purified Protein Derivative), but the thirteenth was scared of the needle! This man had no problem with one shot for heroin, but could not handle the one for the test. We spent about a half an hour before he finally agreed to it. All his friends were putting pressure on him that he couldn't refuse, and put his hand out and had the PPD done.

One patient was an alcoholic and a heroin user. He had three cavities in his lungs from tuberculosis, so I sent him off to a city hospital. After that, I did not see him for six or seven months. Finally, he came to see me again with a case of asthma for which I had previously treated him. He had been to every city hospital in New York City for his tuberculosis. The last hospital he was at was Bellevue, where he was kept in the prison ward because he wouldn't take his medicine for tuberculosis (TB). It took six months before he agreed to take his medication. I took care of his asthma and said, "By the way I would like to have you come in tomorrow for some medicine for your TB." So he said, "Okay." I bought a bottle of whiskey, and told the pharmacist, "Tomorrow when he comes in give him aniacin, persantin and thirty milligrams of whiskey (a shot) and do that every time he comes in." To make a long story short, he never missed a dose. Nine months later his lungs were absolutely clear with no trace of tuberculosis anywhere. And every so often, I would see him lying in the gutter drunk, and I wonder whether I did the right thing or not. But, at least people aren't going to get tuberculosis from him.

HIV (Human Immunodeficiency Virus)

An important priority with HIV patients was that they received their medication and stopped spreading HIV. If a little cocaine persuaded them to come in for their medication, then I was okay with that. What's more important? They are going to get their cocaine anyway. When they come they get a small dose of cocaine. I wasn't in the teaching program. Thousands of lives are saved by getting people to come in and giving them their injection. They are not highly educated. A little bit of heroin, cocaine or whiskey and they take the medicine which prevents them from spreading the disease.

War Club

I had a patient who was going to Tanzania, a small country on the right side of the Middle of Asia. He brought me a Tanzanian war club. The club is very heavy with a ball on the end and the user of the club usually aims to hit the temple lobe where the skull is not that thick. He was in the FBI and had investigated the bombing of the Embassy at Tanzania.

The Party

I once had a man that had a problem with his heart, but he went on a diet and followed it for some time. After three years of following this regime, his heart condition had improved dramatically. Then he decided he is going to have a party in his home on a Thursday. He had filet mignon and apple pie with ice cream; both of which he was not supposed to eat. On Saturday, he came in for his regular bi-monthly visit and his results were still quite good. The following Monday, he went on vacation with his cholesterol still at a fine level. But when he was in Florida for ten days, he continued to break his diet. He came back and, lo and behold, his cholesterol was sky high leaving him in bad shape. After he was back about one week, he had a heart attack and died. That's the price he paid for going off his diet.

By-Pass

I had a patient named Ely, who was in the Robert Wood Johnson Hospital in New Brunswick. They were going to do bypass surgery on him the next day. I found out and went over to the hospital, and I told him, "You don't need to have that surgery and if you keep on the way you are going, you will have to do it over again in about eight or nine years." He was a little afraid of the surgeon, who expected to operate on him and then blackmailed him by saying, "If you don't have this operation then you're going to have to pay yourself for all the time you've been in the hospital. You owe $11,000. You are stuck with it." I then told him that insurance would pay for it whether he had the operation or not. As a matter of fact, they would be happy to have him avoid the operation because **"it"** would save them a lot of money. On Friday at 7:00 in the evening, he got his courage and signed himself out against the advice of the surgeon. Then he saw me. I put him on a diet and told him to exercise, and stop smoking. That was nine years ago; currently he is doing very, very well. He is not going back to his old habits. He is sticking to the diet and his children are very happy with the good shape their father is in.

The mortality rate from surgery runs around five percent or one chance in twenty that one will die from the surgery. Eighty percent of people who have this operation will have it repeated in eight or nine years, because they continue with their lifestyle without diet or exercise adjustments and some doctors who operate are not interested in preventing later operations.

Eagle Scouts Badge

One of my patients had a son who had earned a full Eagle Scout badge. He was to be given the badge at a meeting held in a church located in Hopewell, New Jersey, which is near Princeton. Toward the end of the meeting they asked: "Will all of you who have earned an Eagle Scouts badge please stand up?" About fifty people were at the meeting and only five others stood up. A large number said "Oh, Dr. Seed!!!"

Harvard Reunion 1945. John and Ruth

My Father's Family

Seed is an Irish name. When the British conquered the Irish in 1602, they assigned names to all the local residents. The names were Brown, Green, Apple, Seed, etc and while most of the Irish kept the Celtic names, some kept their assigned names. Those who did were called the black Irish, and migrated to the southern and central areas of the United States around 1730. At the time of the American Revolution they went up to Canada.

Grandfather Seed was a blacksmith and a veterinarian. He made horseshoes, which he then nailed onto the horses' hooves. Grandmother Seed raised silver foxes and minks and brought the furs to the markets. It was hard to make ends meet in those days.

After fifty years on the prairie, grandfather and grandmother Seed retired to the coast of Oregon and gave their farm to their daughter, Tad, and her husband, a former football player for the Chicago team. After two years in Oregon, grandfather Seed said, "I'm going back to North Dakota, where winters are winters and summers are summers". He said, "It isn't summer unless it's over a hundred degrees and it isn't winter unless it's below thirty degrees". On the Oregon coast it was down to forty degrees in winter and up to eighty-five degrees in the summer. He went back to North Dakota to stay with their daughter, Tad and her husband, who had the farm, while grandmother Seed stayed in Oregon. After two years, my grandfather had to have prostate surgery, and grandmother Seed came back to North Dakota and stayed on the same farm. The day before grandfather Seed's operation, he suffered a heart attack and died. Five months later grandmother Seed died of a brain tumor. The two are buried together on the Dakota prairies where they lived together all their adult lives.

My father, Lindon Seed, was born in Wallaceburg, Canada; which was forty miles north of Detroit, in Ontario, Canada on December 10, 1897. When he was a year old, his family moved to Winnipeg, Manitoba, Canada; which is west and above Lake Superior. He had three siblings. The second one was his brother Jack, who worked on the railroad, and was dyslexic, causing him to have some trouble with language. However, apparently he was quite intelligent, because two of his grandchildren went to Harvard College and a third, Huckleberry Seed, went to the California Institute of Technology (Caltech) for the first year and then became a famous poker player. My father's sister, Aunt Mary, was the third child and she stayed at home and took care of the house, while Aunt "Tad", my father's youngest sibling, became a laboratory technician. She lived with my family for two years as she learned the trade at the University of Chicago. She was lots of fun. One day she asked me if I could wiggle my ears. I tried and sure enough, I could wiggle my ears! She also taught me to whistle.

When my father was four years old, the family moved from Winnipeg, Manitoba, Canada to North Dakota. There were rocks piled three to four feet high around the house. As a result of a policy to increase Western settlements, their new house entitled them to own the square mile of land on which it was built. The West had been divided into square miles and anyone who improved a square mile was entitled to own it. This was done to encourage people to move to the west and live in that area. Over time, roads were built on the boundaries of the square miles.

Starting at the age of four, my father on horseback had to pull a sled with a big barrel behind him to get the only source of drinking water, which was two miles away. He would fill up the barrel with water every day and take it back to the house. I have seen pictures of the house. There were rocks around the base, piled up three to four feet high, holding the house in place against the winds. When the weather hit thirty degrees below zero, he carried a hot water bottle under his clothing to pour down the well to melt the ice, so he could pump the water up into the barrel. My father didn't mind when the weather was fifty below zero or colder, because there generally was no wind and more importantly, no school.

When my father was six years old he went to a school in which all the grades from 1st thru 8th were housed in one building with a single teacher. The school was two miles away from home with no roads leading the way, so all the children rode horses by themselves and carried their own books and lunches. There was a large barn attached to school for the horses. There was food for the horses in the barn. On the way back home, the children didn't have to pay much attention, since the horses knew their way home.

When I was eight years old my parents sent me by train to see my grandparents in Minot, North Dakota. They were having severe grasshoppers everywhere. When driving a car, one had to stop and clear out the radiator every thirty minutes for there would be a solid mass of grasshoppers covering it. Looking up at the sun was easy. It would be a white spot in the sky. Before getting into the house the grasshoppers had to be cleaned off the screen.

My Father's School

My father's mother, who was Scottish, wanted to see her son go to the University of North Dakota in Fargo, which was on the border of Minnesota. Unfortunately, the University President did not think that my father was suited for a college education. For one, his table manners were not very good. However, his mother was a political boss in Bottineau and she told the University President that his job was not to decide whether or not her son was fit for education. His job was solely to educate him. So, they admitted him. He was very good in all the academic subjects: literature, mathematics, poetry, etc. He also was very good in athletics: football, basketball and baseball. He was one of the best in each of these sports. In his senior year he became the president of the Iota club, the best of the dormitory clubs. The Iota club was a fraternity comprised solely of male students where they slept and ate. The students had a major influence on how the club was run. One day, he and three of his friends decided to propose marriage to their girlfriends, and whoever was accepted by his girlfriend had to buy beer for the rest. This meant driving over the Red River, the border between North Dakota and Minnesota, to the city of Moorhead where alcohol was legal. Liquor was not legal in North Dakota at that time. None of these men's proposals were accepted. They nevertheless got together and drank a lot of beer. My father assigned two junior students to guard the left over beer which was hidden under his bed. When he woke up in the morning, he discovered drunken freshmen running around on campus and the beer under his bed was gone. This was on a Sunday morning two weeks before the end of the spring term and the end of the university's school year. While the University President and his wife were going to church they saw all these men running around. They also saw my father on his way to work as the clerk in the cafeteria. He usually took a shortcut by jumping over a small brook that was one foot deep. That day he failed and he ended up getting wet. When he got to the cafeteria during the mornings events, he could not figure out how much each student's food cost. He only knew that the average amount was $1.13, so that was what everyone ended up paying for that day, regardless of what they bought. The University President discharged my father from the University after that incident. The University President refused to give him any credit for his current work in that semester for reports he wrote. The Director of Finance for the North Dakota school system was my father's friend, was a very wealthy man and was very important in running the finances of the school system. He must have talked to the University President about my father, and this calmed the president, which resulted in the University President changing my father's punishment allowing my father full credit for what he did. He did not graduate that year, yet he had the highest average of any student. He did graduate a year later. My father's grades were the highest of anybody who had ever attended that university. Seventeen years later, he was granted his Phi Beta Kappa award and had his graduation which included a medal and my father gave both to my mother. She had both made into fashionable earrings which she wore around the universities.

During his last two years of college, my father thought of becoming an airplane pilot. My mother thought he should become a doctor. However, that would have been financially impossible so, unbeknownst to all my mother got her father to give the parents of my father $2,000, so they could give it to their son to go to medical school. I learned of this only after both of my parents had died. My father started his studies at Rush Medical College in 1914.

My Father's Work

In 1917, my father got the job of taking care of medical problems of prisoners in the Bridewell Penitentiary in Chicago during the night from 8:00 pm to 8:00 am. The job was pursued by students from the Rush Medical College who were in their fourth year. Desperately in need of money, my father lied about his education and said he was in his fourth year, when in fact he was only in his third year. Nevertheless, he got the job and it paid well. In his two years working at the Bridewell Penitentiary he became acquainted with a large number of the gangsters in Chicago. That was the time of the notorious Al Capone gangster and his group. My father had a good relationship with all of them, which was useful when he started to practice medicine in Chicago after he had earned his Medical Degree. His office, car and home were never touched.

In the fall of his fourth year at the Rush Medical College, my father was drafted into the Canadian Army. He was born in Canada and hence a Canadian citizen. He had not applied for United States citizenship and so he was drafted into the Canadian Army in the last month of World War I in 1918. The Canadian recruits with whom he lived were lodged in a large four story building in Canada with doors that were locked after 11:00 p.m. One evening my father was late in getting into the building and picked the lock to get in. The following day the captain in charge of the building looked over the records and noticed that my father was not in the building at 11:00 p.m., but was there in the morning. The captain asked him, "Who let you in last night?" My father answered, "No one." The captain said, "Someone must have let you in." My father said, "I picked the lock." The captain said, "You can't do that, the lock is pick proof." My father replied, "Whether it is pick proof or not, I picked it." The captain insisted, "Someone must have let you in." My father got tired of him and said, "Look, the best safecracker in Chicago taught me how to break locks." My father was put into jail for six days and then World War I was over and he was let out of jail and allowed to return to Chicago in 1918. After the war was over he became a United States Citizen.

My Mother's Family

My maternal grandmother's maiden name was Griffin, a typical Welsh name. Wales is a wide peninsula west of England separated by a channel from Northern Ireland. My maternal grandfather's name was Frederick William Cathro and my great-grandfather was Peter Cathro. This is a Scottish lowland level landsman name. Those of this status were typically lowland level farmers, while the highland level landsmen were horseback riding nomads with names like McCarthy or MacDonald. The nomads often killed wild animals for food, but they occasionally also raided the lowland level farmers. In the battles that followed, the low level landsmen fought back with spears shouting: "Thrust and Caa Through My Men". A group of men who were particularly adept at killing the high landsmen were given the name "Caa Through". "Caa" meant "cut" and "Caa Through" evolved in time to the modern surname "Cathro".

In 1933, my grandfather Cathro had a meeting with the Mandan Indians who mainly lived in Manitoba, Canada. The ceremony was held at the automobile racetrack in Bottineau, North Dakota. There were about a hundred people there and they were dressed in ordinary Western business clothes. From ten in the morning to two in the afternoon, there were talks and signings. Everybody was a Mandan, except my grandfather and me. I was about one hundred yards away from where the meeting was being held. I was eleven years old and I was absolutely bored. Later on, I asked my grandfather why they had the ceremony with the Mandan Tribe, but I never got a straight answer. The Mandan's were getting up and sitting down but in no pattern. There were sections of eight people who could be getting up and going down to talk, but there was no particular order in which they were coming down. Probably the most likely reason was that every year my grandfather sent about 1,500 head of cattle to Chicago, which would be hard to do without help. He may have hired the Mandan's to act as his cowboys and paid them well for it. He died in 1934 and I never heard the whole story. He was a very stern man who wasn't very talkative. I don't think I ever heard him laugh.

In 1904 it was quite unusual for people to own cars. I have a picture of my mother driving one at Lake Metigoshe, a lake that is half in Canada and half in the United States. My father told us that at one time, grandfather Cathro owned 35% of the land in North Dakota. However, there were five successive years of drought, during which he lost an enormous amount of money and land. He also set up the banking system for the state of North Dakota, directed it and had been respectably praised for it since then. The state of North Dakota is the only state where banking policy is controlled by the vote of the Senate. There were also several newspaper reports about William Cathro helping the school system in Bottineau.

The Cathro's lived out on the prairie about twelve to twenty years before the Seeds. Grandfather F.W. Cathro went back 1,074 miles east to Ann Arbor, Michigan to attend the University of Michigan to earn his Bachelor's degree, and then returned back to the Dakota Prairies.

After returning home, my father's great-grandmother told him about the time when a Mandan Indian came to attack the settlers during his great-grandfather's absence. From the family's house near Bismarck, his great-grandmother could see the Indian approaching from a distance. She and the children ran up the ladder of the water tower, which was about twenty-five feet high and was next to their house. They stayed in the water tower and did not make a bit of noise. The Indian had come to steal and kill, but couldn't find signs of where anyone was hidden, despite searching underneath the floors and throughout the house. About two or three hours later, he still couldn't find anybody, so he went away. Then my great grandmother and her children came out of the water tower.

My great grandfather Cathro helped write the Constitution for North Dakota in 1876. He and some friends in North Dakota helped to put together a constitution and submitted it to Congress. Congress decided to grant North Dakota to be a state and then decided to use the same constitution for South Dakota statehood at the same time. After North Dakota became a state, they set up the school system for the state which Frederick Cathro helped supervise for the next thirty years.

My Mother: Frances Cathro

At the time my father was admitted to the University of North Dakota, he met a sophomore woman. She felt that he was a very smart young man and decided that she was going to be his girl! Later, she married him. My mother's name was Frances Lorene Cathro.

She was the second of three daughters: Helen, Frances and Marian Cathro. Aunt Helen lived on the outskirts of Minot, North Dakota. She was stern and rigid; I never saw her smile. Aunt Marian was a pleasant school teacher in Aberdeen, Idaho. Her husband held the superintendent position of the school system. Aunt Marian and her husband, Uncle Roy, lived in Aberdeen, Idaho which was the only home at the edge of a huge flat plain. The plain desert was where potatoes were grown. They also had a place ninety miles from Aberdeen in the mountains, three miles from the Lava Hot Springs, and 1,000 feet higher. Lava Hot Springs was a city of 520 people who live 129 miles north of Salt Lake City, Utah. The Lava Hot Springs produces three million gallons of water a day at a temperature of 102° to 112°. It is at an elevation of 5,020.

My mother was a very good housekeeper. Anything around that wasn't important, was thrown out. My mother was a very good cook. There were a lot of women who wanted to know her recipes. She would give them the recipe, but she would always alter a small part of it. She didn't want anybody to be able to make the food the same way she could do it. One of the things that my mother did that was good at Christmas time, was a cookie that had a thick paste of dates in the center, and was covered with an almond flavor. It was terrific. I used to ask my mother how she made them. She wouldn't tell me, year after year, decade after decade, I asked about the recipe. Finally my mother was in her seventies, she said, "John, I've forgotten how I made them". It was a terrific way of making cookies, and my mother forgets it! Tragedy! She was known to other women for her cooking. She majored in cooking at the University of North Dakota and had a master's degree in Nutrition. My mother also did pottery work at the University of North Dakota. Eventually all the pottery broke one way or another.

One fine day my mother found a red lipstick stain on the neck of my father's shirt. She began asking questions of how it got there. There was a young woman training to be a surgeon and had kissed my father. My mother went to the hospital and gave her a talk the following day; she chewed her out. She told her that he was her husband and she had better stay away. After that the young woman's ability to work with my father was very limited.

John's sister, Linda, and our mother

My mother always claimed that gambling was immoral. When I was raised I was taught that gambling was sinful. When World War II came along, my father volunteered to join the army. He went to help build a hospital for the military in central Illinois. At Christmas time he came home from central Illinois and after a few days in Oak Park he left to go back. I was driving him to catch the local elevated train to get to the regular train from Chicago to go back to central Illinois. My mother was standing in the back porch and called out, "Are you sure that you have enough money for the poker game"? My father replied, "Yes", and I drove off. I said "I thought that poker playing was immoral". My father replied, "It's only immoral if you lose". My father played a lot of poker when he was at the Mayo Clinic, and usually lost. My mother eventually persuaded him to stop because they could not afford it, it was immoral. But when he had come back from central Illinois to see my mother, she found out that he had more money in the pockets of his pants than could be accounted for by his salary. Then poker had become moral!

My Parents' Marriage - August 17, 1920

My father married my mother in her home in Bottineau, North Dakota at noon on August 17, 1920 and about fifty guests were present. Among them was my grandfather, Dr. D.F. Seed and my mother's father, Fred Cathro. It is not clear that my grandmother was there. My mother's mother was there, along with a brother of my father and my mother's two sisters, who also lived in Bottineau. My mother's sister Marian was the maid of honor. My father's best man was Vernon Miller, and Rev. I.D. McBain performed the ceremony. After the ceremony, they drove to Grand Forks and then on Route 2 to Duluth, Minnesota where they caught a boat on Lake Superior to Chicago, Illinois where they planned to live. I was born two years after my parents were married.

Rush Medical College was taken over by the University of Illinois - College of Medicine in 1919. The surgery department was taken over by four doctors; Lindon Seed, Charles H. Phifer, Arrie Bamberger and Ralph Charles Sullivan. They were known as "The Four Horsemen" and legends in the history of the University of Illinois - College of Medicine. Their constant oral quizzes, given twice a week on an assigned number of pages, in addition to a monthly written examination, sent a chill down the spines of students' backs. The students took the day off before the written examination. The other professors protested over this because the students were skipping their lesson in order to pass the exam. This lasted during the 1920's and on to the 30's. I had occasionally met doctors who had been students of my father. When they met me they all told me what a good teacher he was and what a good physician he was.

My father who at the age of seventy-seven still practiced at Grant Hospital in Chicago said, "I quizzed those boys on everything, essentially the fine print . . . . and let me tell you, my students read the book. It was an effective teaching method." The textbook used by the Department of Surgery back then was "Rose and Carless, Manual of Surgery". There were practically no textbooks worth anything at that time. In fact there were no others. When he graduated from Rush Medical College in 1919, there were no residencies in Chicago. So he went to Mayo Clinic in Minnesota for his residency. "That tells you something about the quality of medical education," he said. He felt that there was no medical education of any use. Students could apply to the University of Illinois's College of Medicine in 1926 with two years of pre-medical work at the University of Illinois's Urbana-Champaign Campus, including the satisfactory completion of a set number of high school and college units in such courses as English, Biology, Physics, Chemistry, a foreign language, etc. The curriculum of the college consisted then of two years of pre-clinical work and one year as an intern at a hospital approved by the University. The reason that quizzes were necessary in those days was because of the quality of the students. My father said, "A student's love of academic training was a lot of hokum, etc". As the quality of the students at the college improved over the years, the need for quizzes subsided, but "he still had to hold a club over their heads to get them to study," he said.

No one took roll call back then, but the "Four Horsemen" did. My father asserted, "And let me tell you, those students came to class and they read the book!" According to him, the school closed down the day before the "Four Horsemen" had their monthly written quiz. Students cut their classes and stayed home to study. The other faculty members would complain about us because of this. My father added, "Let me tell you, that monthly examination kept those boys on the beam . . . we didn't flunk many students back then."

Anus of the Carnes

My mother wanted to belong to the wealthy social society in North Chicago but my father did not. One day my mother and father were invited to an elegant party by one of the people in that group. After the meal, each couple told a story about something unusual they had done or encountered. When it came to my parents, my father told them about how he helped his father, a veterinarian, take the temperature of a cow. He described chewing a cud of tobacco until the mouth was full of saliva, then pulling up the tail of the cow to spit at the anus of the cow. He then put a thermometer into the rectum and watched the mercury come up. The men present laughed wildly, whereas the women were sitting up stiff with a stern look of disapproval. My parents were never invited again. My mother had to settle for socializing with doctors and their families. Since then, they weren't invited to any other high social parties.

During his career to be a doctor in the area around Chicago and Indianapolis my father had the opportunity to see his girlfriend, who later became his wife. He liked to see her on weekends when he could, if he was able to get the chance to drive down there to Indianapolis. One Saturday morning, a gangster, who had broken his hip the evening before, needed an operation that would last until noon at Rush University Hospital. My father was annoyed to have to stay that long and told the gangster that the time of his operation would require more time and was interfering with seeing his wife in Indianapolis. While he was in the operating room the gangster brought out his car keys. This was astonishing. In the operating room patients are not supposed to have anything with them except for minimal hospital clothing. The gangster gave his keys to my father and told him where his car was parked. After the operation was over my father went out and found the car exactly where the gangster said it would be. He soon found he had a car that could go at hundred miles per hour at a time when no other cars including police cars, could go more than sixty miles per hour. My father arrived in Indianapolis on time and had a car to drive around in with his wife.

My father applied for an appointment at the Cook County Hospital in Chicago, Illinois. He had to take a written examination before he could do surgical procedures on his own. In the examination, age counted for fifty percent. My father was the youngest doctor to ever get an appointment there. With that appointment he automatically became a professor at the University of Illinois. Soon, his practice increased rapidly. He became the doctor for the patients on the floor of Cook County Hospital where the criminals were housed. He knew many of them personally from the two years he had worked at the Bridewell Penitentiary. One time when he was making rounds with some of the students from the University of Illinois, he stopped in front of one patient and told the students about the stealing of the silver from a house one block down the street where we lived. While the students were there, my father said "Wasn't that too bad," the students agreed and things went along. The next Saturday that house was broken into and the silver was replaced. There was nothing ever stolen from my father's car or from our house.

Two years after his fourth year at the Rush Medical College, he applied for training as a surgeon at the Mayo Clinic in Rochester, Minnesota because there was no training in surgery at the Rush Medical College or any other school in Chicago at that time. He asked Rush Medical College to transmit a copy of his grades to the Mayo Clinic before he had an interview there for a surgical internship. The appointment was on a weekend but since Rush Medical College did not transmit the records until the next week, he was told at Mayo Clinic that they would have to cancel his appointment. I suspect that his social graces were not too good and this worked against him. He was not accepted and took the train back to Chicago. When he arrived home, there was a telegram inviting him to go to the Mayo Clinic in Rochester, Minnesota. His transcript had arrived. He had the highest grades of anybody in his class. The Mayo Clinic recognized that they had made a mistake, and my father received the internship, which started on January 1, 1921 and ended January 1, 1924.

Two doctors, who were brothers, started the Mayo clinic. One was Charles Mayo and the other William Mayo. The second was much more able than the first brother. One day while my father was operating with Charles Mayo, he noticed an error and he corrected it without making any fuss. William Mayo reviewed the reports on all of the operations and noticed this error. He invited my father to explain what happened and appreciated that my father had covered it up. He also saw to it that whenever my father came to Rochester, Minnesota his hotel bills were paid for by the Mayo Clinic. Later, my father became the President of the Mayo Clinic Alumni Association and remained President for a number of years.

After his three years at the Mayo Clinic my father returned to Chicago to work at the Presbyterian Hospital. On his trip back from the Mayo Clinic, my father stopped by to see me at the Harvard Massachusetts Hospital, where I was an intern. I advised him to use iodine for people with thyroid disease. I even suggested that he should go to Oak Ridge, Tennessee to learn how to use radioactive iodine. He eventually went to Oak Ridge, Tennessee and learned about using the radioactive iodine. He continued working at the Rush Presbyterian Hospital and at Grant Hospital in Chicago, despite the fact that they were six miles apart.

Water in Upper Mississippi River

My father went out to visit friends in North Dakota at the end of World War II. He was astounded because he had never seen much grass. There were ravines covered in green bushes and trees. There were no swarms of grasshoppers. The government had made dams and rivers from the Rocky Mountains in western Montana which caused water from the lakes at the beginning of the Mississippi River in Montana, twenty years earlier, to evaporate and then later causing rain in North Dakota. That environment was well suited for the development of green plants.

Thyroid Treatment

When my father was at the Mayo Clinic, an internal medicine doctor there discovered that if one administered patients with iodine deficiency with large amounts of iodine prior to thyroid surgery, the patients recovered better and faster than if they were given nothing. Without the iodine ahead of time the mortality rate was 10% to 15%. With prior iodine treatment the mortality rate was about 0.6%. When my father left the Mayo Clinic he came to work in Chicago and started doing thyroid surgery at the Grant Hospital Chicago, Illinois. All the other doctors in Chicago didn't believe in the use of iodine. My father's thyroid surgery was done at a private hospital, the Grant Hospital, which is one mile above the north branch of the Chicago River and at the Cook County hospital which is 6.4 miles south of the Grant Hospital. The Presbyterian Hospital didn't use iodine.

The Invention of Cold Blood Transfusion

While my father was operating at the Cook County Hospital, he became aware of how difficult it was to give blood transfusions. This was at the time that Al Capone was active and was having a war with other gangs. A lot of people were being shot and needed transfusions of blood. One would try to find someone who had the same blood type as the patient, and then put him in a chair or a stretcher with his right arm on the same side as the patient's left arm or vice versa. Then with a large syringe, pull out some blood from the donor's vein and inject it into the patient's vein. They would continue to do this over and over again until they got enough blood into the patient. My father had the idea that it would be a lot better if one could collect a large amount of cold blood and store it for future use. So he researched to find out how long one can store cold blood and under what conditions. He checked out differences between bloods. Fortunately, the people at the Rockefeller Institute in New York, New York, had worked out all of the reactions that could occur between different blood types, but had not thought about storing large amounts for future use and keeping it cold. My father worked out all of the details: the type of blood of the donor and the receptor, the shape of the glass containers, the size of the tubing for the administering of the blood, the set up, how it would be stored cold and how it was to be used. What happened to blood if one saved it? What was the best temperature? If stored cold, how long could it be saved? It turned out to be a month. And was extra salt in it needed? Infection in the blood did not occur if one was careful. That was the beginning of blood banks. Finally all this was done and a supply of it was put in the gallery with a glass front and instructions on it. It was posted at the Cook County Hospital on Thursday, November 11, 1929. Cold blood banks were invented by Lindon Seed, MD. My youngest brother Randolph Seed has the announcement.

In addition to working at the Cook County Hospital, my father had a private practice at the Grant Hospital in Chicago's north side. In the spring of 1930 the American Medical Association (the AMA based in Chicago) was opposing the government's attempt to begin Medicare. One day *The Chicago Tribune* newspaper had a headline on the front page reading, "Dr. Seed Favors Medicare". Although my father was a member of the AMA, he did not agree with the AMA and he was so well known that the Chicago Tribune used his outlook to let people know how he felt. Fortunately, Medicare was adopted!

Home Garden Contest

My father had no avocation until a patient gave him a gardenia plant. He put it into the ground in the backyard and he paid no attention to it. One month later when that same patient saw my father again, he asked how the gardenia plant was doing. My father told him that it had died. The patient said, "Died? You can't kill a gardenia." My father was upset. He was given a new gardenia plant and started to do gardening. About two years later, he had a patient who needed thyroid surgery. It was a school teacher who did not have enough money to pay for surgery, but she had a son who was finishing a college program for a degree in landscaping. My father offered surgery in turn for landscaping. My father did a good operation and her son did a good job of the landscaping. I did a lot of digging for my father. Five years after my father began gardening, the Oak Park City started having a prize for the house that had the best landscape. Five years in a row he won. The village then refused to let him enter the contests anymore. It all started when I became his gardener, and dug holes for plants and bushes. One day he had a bush he wanted to move. He was trying to do it himself and had been digging around it, but he couldn't move it. He then called me to help him. He was going to pull on one side and wanted me to pull from the other side. I said, "Why don't you step back, Dad, and let me pull it alone." I then grabbed the bush and pulled it until it came out easily. He then realized from then on he could no longer spank me without my permission.

The Board of Directors at the Grant Hospital had appointed my father to be the director of the surgery department. All went well until the time came when one of the surgeons had lost a lot of his abilities and his patients were not doing well. My father encouraged him to stop doing certain operations, but he refused. The trustees backed that doctor and insisted on allowing him to do all the different types of surgery he wanted to perform, due to the fact that he had a large practice and was bringing in a lot of patients. The board refused to agree with my father and so my father stepped down and was no longer the director. However, my father had a large practice and from that point on, he insisted on operating when he wanted to, regardless of, when the other doctors wanted to operate. This marked a change in his attitude. When he was a director, he felt obliged to let others operate when they wanted to operate, but now he no longer felt that way. He did not step aside for the other doctors anymore.

Hospital in England

During the early stages of World War II, although my father was not a US citizen, he volunteered to serve in the United States Army and was very committed to the United States army. The army was wondering if they would need another hospital in England. They started to build the hospital in Southern Illinois and my father was assigned to build it. When the army decided to make the new hospital for southern England, my father requested that all the soldiers assigned to work in the army hospital would be men who could be tailors before they came into the army. Many of the men had been with him in Southern Illinois. He had requested these men to be tailors so that they could make as much of the clothing required for the hospital supplies as possible. It was to be built in the midlands of southern England. They loaded the hospital on a ship and unloaded it in England. My father watched carefully as they unloaded the ship that carried all the parts. He set up a tent on the dock where the ship was being unloaded for his tailors to work making all the clothing needed for the hospital and operating rooms. On the dock the regular soldiers came and gave the sewing soldiers their food all day and night. When he saw that they were unloading a four foot square box that carried thread, he said to the soldier unloading the ship, "Put that over here, it is for the hospital supply". The soldier doing the unloading work was not an officer, therefore he did as ordered. My father knew from his experience in Illinois that the official amount of thread that was supplied was not enough to make all of the clothing for the soldiers who had no arms, hands, feet, legs, etc who needed surgery. The box being carried with thread was needed for all over England. After he had taken all he needed, he then let England have the thread they needed.

While the work was going on under the tent, an American boat had sunken in the ocean. That boat carried many typewriters for use by the army headquarters in London.

My father felt that headquarters in Boston needed to send somebody to come and get the hospital typewriters so that he had someone sitting on the typewriters and they prevented London from getting them. There were only four typewriters on the sunken boat that were to be used for hospital supplies. When part of the supplies for the hospital arrived two days earlier, my father suspected that headquarters would look to see if his boat with the hospital supplies had any typewriters. They did have four typewriters in their supplies. Headquarters in London came to get them. Headquarters sent one of their top people to go to the port where hospital supplies were being unloaded. My father assigned soldiers to sit on top of the typewriters and supplies and not to let anybody take them and not to leave them unguarded at any time. The top general from London came and said that he was taking the four typewriters. The sergeant said, "You can not take them sir. My officer said that no one is to take these". The General asked, "Who is your officer?" The sergeant said, "Colonel Seed." The General asked, "Where is he?" The sergeant replied, "I don't know sir." He then went around looking for Colonel Seed and could not find him. Everybody was advised not to know the whereabouts of Colonel Seed. The General from London went back to London empty handed!

The time allotted to get the hospital operating was ten days after the boat landed in port. The previous record was thirty days for a hospital that size, anywhere before, under any conditions. In this case, a regular army physician was in charge. He took charge of orders for supplies and reports. He left all medical things to my father. As much as my father liked to do surgery, he never did any while he was in the army. However, he did oversee and review each patient who came to the hospital. He then decided which doctor would care for each patient and which doctor would perform any surgery. There were seventeen wings to the hospital and eighty soldiers in each wing. He saw all soldiers in one wing every week.

My father had a bet of seventy cents that he could find some mistake somewhere in their wing. One day the army physicians from a particular wing thought everything was perfect. One soldier had a bullet going through the upper part of the right forearm. My father asked the soldier to make a fist of that arm and then the left little finger, but the soldier could not move a normal amount. The reason for this abnormal movement was because one out of ten people have the nerve to that finger in an unusual course. In this case the bullet went into the area of the nerve. This nerve was hard to find and almost never heard of. Every visit was a challenge, but yet a pleasant one.

Ten years after the war, one of the surgeons that had served under my father became a professor at Harvard University. He came to see me at my tenth reunion with my colleagues at the Massachusetts Hospital of Harvard University, and he said to me, "It was an honor to work under your father."

The army hospital was built in two directions at ninety degree angles. At the inside of the intersection there was a big tent. At the intersection where they joined was where his office was and on the other part of the intersection was where the administrator was located. Out of my father's window there was big tent. Nobody asked about it. Inside there were spades, shovels, lawn mowers, etc.; everything that was available back home was also available there. He had the soldiers cutting the grass, trimming bushes, planting the flowers, etc.

One day my father was at a meeting of doctors in England who were involved in comparing information and ideas on what should be done with injured soldiers coming in from other sites in England. It was Friday, when the meeting was over, the doctors were leaving and they happened to go by a storage site, where they could see very nice black plastic rolls of material. My father noticed this and went to the administrator of his unit and he inquired about getting some of those rolls. The administrator agreed to his request. He needed a truck, a car and five soldiers. He needed to get them some material to put down on the corridors of his hospital. The administrator agreed on what he wanted to do and he obtained some additional help.

At around 4:30 am they arrived to this storage site. My father arrived in a car. The truck was parked out of sight and it was still dark outside. My father asked the soldier at the entrance, "Can I take some of the corridor rolls?" The man said, "Yes, take everything you want, I am going to have breakfast now." My father signaled the truck to come into sight and they took all that they could and drove off.

The hospital had lovely corridors with this covering. They also had lovely lawns, walks and flowers. All the soldiers took great pride in their hospital. They knew they were the best medically, as well as the best in appearance.

Six months later my father happened to be at this same storage site, and the same fellow was in charge and asked, "Were you the one who was here six months ago?" My father replied, "Yes." The man said, "You took almost everything. I didn't know you had a big truck." My father said, "Well, you told me to take everything I wanted."

When the war was over and my father was back in the United States, he looked around before he went back to work. He noticed that a building was being put up that would be one hundred levels high. The high skyscraper was near the water front of Lake

Michigan. He contacted them about having an office at the twenty-second level which lets one look out over a part of Lake Michigan. My father talked with me often, near Lake Michigan, when he came back from the war.

He wanted to work with radioactive iodine and to do this he had to use lead pipes. Radioactive iodine had to go down through lead pipes that prevented any radioactivity to get into any of the offices all the way down. He did it and it worked.

At the age of seventy my father ceased doing any surgery, but maintained his office practice till he was eighty-one and worked until the last two months of his life. In the course of his career he did approximately 7,000 thyroid operations and practiced for sixty years.

Locusts

For several weeks when I was out in Minot, North Dakota in 1932, when I was ten years old, there were so many locusts in the air that looking at the sun was like looking at a full moon at night, except that the background was lighter. The locusts acted viciously, leaving no green plants or trees anywhere. If a broom with a wooden pole was left outdoors, it would be transformed into a very rough pole from locusts trying to eat it. When driving a car, the driver would have to stop every hour to brush the locusts off the radiator. When entering the house, one first brushed the locusts off the door and hurried to get inside. This lasted for several weeks.

Cactus

My memory of Aunt Helen when I was nine years old, I went to visit her in Minot, North Dakota. I was walking around barefoot next to her house, which was covered solid with cacti that were as high as twenty feet. One day I walked barefoot and the spikes of cactus penetrated the bottom of my feet. I came back and I couldn't walk for three days.

Packrats

Aunt Marian and Uncle Roy Weston lived in Aberdeen, in the center of the large flat area for Idaho potato production. Aunt Marian was a school teacher and her husband was the school principal. They also had a summer place high in the mountains about three miles from Lava Hot Springs and thirty-five miles from their home. The first time driving up the path to their summer house, I was very anxious. About a foot and half from the edge of the road, there was a thousand foot drop. At the bottom there was a beautiful beaver dam with clear water. The track was bumpy and rough to drive over, and about a half a mile was covered in weeds. Uncle Roy made a sharp left turn to a small cabin. There were packrats running across the roof all night. They would find something that had a bright color, take it to their nest, and put something back in its place, like a nut.

Beaver's Den

Five years later, my brothers and I, drove up to the mountains near Hot Springs. Randy was driving and Richard was sitting with me in the back seat. It was a narrow trail and there was a slope of ninety degrees down the side to where the beavers den was and that was about a thousand feet down. Richard wanted to know what a beaver's den was like, but he didn't see the den because he was very scared and said, "Randy, watch the trail! Keep your eyes on the road! Randy watch the trail! Randy watch the trail!" Randy was looking at the beaver's den and was admiring the beauty of it. Richard was continually screaming about watching where Randy was driving and he never learned about what a good beaver's den was like. I was with them on these trips and enjoyed it.

Potatoes

Aberdeen, Idaho is twenty five miles to reach, and is at the edge of the large flat desert plain. They send somebody to go up into the mountains of Snake Rivers Plains to test the depths of the snow in four or five places; that told the amount of the water they would get in the spring and how many potatoes that they will be able to plant. When the snow melts this water is guided to pools. When the water is needed it is guided to the soil where the potatoes will be planted. In the town of Aberdeen the snow melts and travels across the plateau in channels, a form of tunnels that keep the water in the soil away from the sun. This reading affects the amount of potatoes to plant. The channels bring water to the different areas of the potatoes. The farmers are informed when the water will come and how much. At the beginning of August the schools begin and run for one month to compensate for the time in October when the schools are closed, so that everybody can help take potatoes out of the ground. During this time, even some offices close for two months to go and collect potatoes. The older children help with digging up the potatoes and some earn enough to get bicycles. Others earned enough to buy a car. The potatoes are put in long, huge half-circle sheds, the length of a football field, twenty feet high and five yards wide. Then they work in the sheds for the next four to five months cleaning the potatoes and treating the skins in an effort to prevent mildew. Finally, the railroad cars are lined with paper and filled with the cleaned potatoes and shipped off to the rest of the United States. They usually shipped off three freight cars per day.

Trip to Idaho
(as recalled by Randy)

Early one Monday morning my uncle Roy and Aunt Marian, their son Bruce, my sister and I all started our trip from Chicago to Idaho. The first day we drove about 320 miles to Rochester, Minnesota. In Rochester, I got lost in the park, I played around the train yards, helped load a freight train, and talked to the train engineers.

We left Rochester and on our way we passed the Mayo Clinic where my father studied medicine and where I was born. The next morning, while riding a bicycle I fell off, and hurt my arm. It had a hard time healing. The next place we went was to Benson, Minnesota past Big Stone Lake in South Dakota.

Benson, Minnesota

I had a grand time swimming, fishing, boating and surf riding. Here I also shot a gun for the first time; I took advantage of this by firing around one hundred shots. I could not have a gun in Chicago because it would be too dangerous. In surf riding, I tried many stunts with two other boys who where there. While there I put hot packs on my arm because of an infection caused by falling off the bike at Benson. On the day we left my uncle was going to Fargo, which was on our way, so we rode with him in the rumble seat of his car until we switched to my other uncle's car. At Fargo, we ate lunch before we left for Bismarck. I had fun for it was new scenery; we were passing the hills of southern North Dakota.

My grandfather Cathro lived in Mandan, North Dakota, which is across the Missouri River from Bismarck. He worked in the courthouse of Bismarck. The evening we arrived, my grandfather took us to the railroad station, where we saw some Indians dancing.

The next day, my grandfather showed us all around Bismarck. We went along the Missouri River and then to the water plant. On our way there, we passed over some hills on which there were small trenches covered with vegetation. These little trenches were forts and lookouts for soldiers fighting Indians a hundred years ago. Along the river on the same trail we drove over in the car. At the water plant, we saw the water as it came in from the Missouri River, how the dirt was made to settle, how it went through the filters, and last of all, the laboratory where they tested the water. We saw a sample of water taken from the river when it was especially dirty. However, the water had all gone to the top leaving the dirt behind.

After this, my grandfather took us to see some people that my aunt and uncle knew. From there, we went to the Weather Bureau. It was interesting and educational. We saw some small delicate instruments that recorded air which indicated if there would be a storm and the activity in the atmosphere. We saw how scientists made charts for temperature and air currents. We watched as a man filled a ten cent balloon with hydrogen, tested it for leaks and found one. He took another and found it to be alright. He took a balloon filled with hydrogen up to a platform on the roof where he released it. He watched it through a stereoscope and talked through a telephone to the man below, who traced its' route and velocity. This is how they find out about the wind.

After this, we went to see them build the new capital building in Bismarck, North Dakota. It is sixteen stories high, the highest building in North Dakota. On coming to Bismarck, it was hilly ground where we couldn't see the city at all. The only thing we could see was this one lonely building ahead of us. It looks rather queer from all sides when seen from a distance. The contractor in charge was a friend of my grandfather's who showed us around and explained how they built it. The following day we started for Lake Metigoshe, which is between Canada and the United States. My grandmother Cathro and my two cousins live there with their mother in the summer time. They have two summer homes.

When I was eight years old the family was visiting at Lake Metigoshe, fifteen miles northeast of Bottineau in the state of North Dakota. Lake Metigoshe is a lake about thirty miles long, that is located half in Canada and half in North Dakota and it is a mile wide at its' widest point. Both sides of the lake were heavily covered with trees about fifty to sixty feet tall. Grandfather Cathro had two summer homes on the west side of the lake and about a mile from the southern end of the lake. The home we saw was about the size of a normal home and about ten yards back from the lake. At the back of the house there was a single car wide path to drive to the home. The grass was six to eighteen inches high and had not been cut. There were only lamps. Water came from a pump outside the house. Fifty yards from the back of the house was the outhouse, where one went to the bathroom to urinate and defecate.

Going out to the lake there was a twelve yard long ramp to the water. Attached to it was a boat. At the end of the ramp there was a small diving board. Out near the end of the pier was the place where my four year old sister threw an aluminum funnel six inches in diameter along the circular top that curves down to a tube with an opening one half an inch in diameter across the bottom opening and cutting sharp. She had thrown it into the water with the narrow tube side up. The bottom landed on the arch of my foot and cut a deep hole into my foot. I had climbed out and my father took care of it. It took about four to five days to heal.

After we left Minot, North Dakota, which was on our way, we came to a strip of road, Route 2, about twenty-five miles long on which nobody lived. There were so many grasshoppers that our windshield was yellow with dead grasshopper stains. All along the road were crops ruined by these pests. We could not see any living green crops because of the huge number of these bugs.

While we were there, I did not miss a day of swimming. Soon, I was able to dive off the tower that was twenty feet high. Also I would go rowing every day, except for one. Sometimes my cousin Fred and I would take trips by rowboat to different parts of the lake. I was sorry to leave.

Upon leaving Bottineau to go to Minot, we came to the same road that had the grasshoppers. My cousin Bruce and I busily engaged ourselves with the job of cleaning out grasshoppers from the radiator of the car. There were about a hundred of them.

The last thing we did before we left Minot was to visit my grandfather and grandmother Seed. They owned a fox farm about one-half mile from Minot. Around the farm there where the following animals: two squirrels, nine dogs (one mother and eight puppies), and fifteen cats. The cats would feed the baby foxes that the mother fox did not take care of. He also has about fifty minks, a hundred silver foxes, some horses, cows and a sheep. Linda, my sister, went walking amongst the pens of foxes and the sheep. While she was walking towards the gate a sheep charged at her. My grandfather helped her through the gate just in time to close it before the sheep rammed into it. He was a little bit ferocious.

When we entered Wyoming, after a long drive, I saw for the first time, a real desert with nothing but cacti growing. The ground was a red color, but some spots had many colors. The real beauty and excitement began at Cody, Wyoming, the first town mentionable on our way to Yellowstone National Park. About half a mile from Cody, we came to a valley and dam. At the dam, on one side it was about ten feet down to the water, and on the other side there was a five hundred foot drop to bare pointed rocks. To make matters worse, the mountains were immense above us. When coming down from Sylvan Pass, we saw a deer pausing to take a good look, but we made some noise and he ran off.

Next we drove around to find a lodging place. The following morning my sister, my cousin, and I just wandered about until we heard somebody say there was a bear at the garbage can. We had lots of fun chasing after him. Every time he looked around at us we would run away as fast as we could. At one cabin, the bear parked on the doorstep because he wanted to get some more food. Luckily, it wasn't our doorstep. After the bear left, we took a stroll along the walking trail. That day we saw six bears, one brown bear and five black ones. We also saw a mother bear with her three cubs. The evening before we found our camp, a mother bear and her cub blocked the road until we gave them some food. The mother bear put her head in the window and my aunt immediately threw out some food and closed the window. That shows how tame the bears were!

At Yellowstone, Old Faithful is a geyser which spurts every hour. We got there just five minutes before it really erupted. First, I saw a grayish white mound of earth in front of the most beautiful scenery. Then, there was a spurt about five feet high that ended up soaring until it went sixty feet into the air. It was a sight to behold of real glory with all of nature's force and beauty.

On our way to Aberdeen, Idaho, from Yellowstone Park we could see the Grand Teton Mountains which were as beautiful as those in Yellowstone. We saw a forest fire far off in the distance. In the hundred miles of desert we passed through, we saw lots of sagebrush. This is a plant that grows without water and has silver gray leaves all the time.

Aberdeen, Idaho

After seeing the Grand Tetons, we went seventy miles south and twenty miles west to see the Darren Mountains and Dempsey Creek which would be seen by the Girl Scouts in two more days. The Grand Tetons could be seen from miles away.

The first day, we helped make the pack trail by clearing away the rocks. All I could see was a bunch of canyons with trees in them that divided and subdivided the area with the Darren Mountains coming up from them and I couldn't tell one from another. We went fishing for trout up on the Big Dempsey Creek. The creek was only three feet wide, but we fished up by the beaver dams where it was forty feet wide and two feet deep. The water was so clear that we could watch the fish come up to our hooks to bite or just nibble. It was interesting to watch the fish.

The day after, I ran one half of the way up a mountain and ran down again. All the activity got me sick, but I wanted to see the sunset from the top. The next day, I helped my uncle build a bathtub and kitchen for the girl scouts who were coming.

Uncle Roy showed us a mountain lion's cave. The lion once lived there, but he had been killed, so a coyote built his home in there. We also found a dead porcupine with all the needles in his hide. The whole cave looked gloomy and frightful, especially after hearing about who lived in it. We left the cave and started to walk towards the mossy terraces, where the stream started that came by our ranch. On our way, we stopped to look at a gold mine and lumber mill. From where we were the gold mine looked like two broken down shacks.

Later, while swimming, some scabs came off from sores I had acquired two weeks ago. One was from falling and the other was from going down on the toboggan with Bruce. While Bruce and I were going down on the toboggan, we agreed to get as far back as we could on it, and Bruce, being in earnest, pushed me back after I had gone as far back as I could. So, I slid down on my buttocks, the rest of the way, with my hands and feet on the toboggan. After the swim, I went to the doctor and he put a bandage on the one I got from the toboggan because it was the worst. We did not want to have to walk amongst the sheep to get to the cabin because it would only start a sheep panic. One day the sheep came and surrounded our cabins and while they were pasturing we would call them names according to the way they talked, like clarinet, trumpet, trombone, etc.

When we got back to the cabin we found my aunt coming up to leave the ranch because Uncle Roy was so sick. We helped them and within six minutes they had left the ranch for Lava Hot Springs, where my uncle saw the doctor. The next day, the doctor said my uncle might have pneumonia. We left for Aberdeen.

While in Aberdeen, I typed a letter to my father. I got on the train and said goodbye to my aunt and uncle who had provided such a good vacation for me. As soon as we got settled I began looking over the places we were going to pass. About then I noticed Lava

Hot Springs, so I prepared to take my last look at it. When I saw it, a peculiar feeling came over me. I wished I could stay there and that I could see all my friends again that had treated me so nicely and say a last goodbye for maybe I will never get to go there again.

Somewhere in the neighborhood there was a den of cubs of one of the mother cougars. She was not hunting for food, so I went out wandering in the area.

My younger brother, Randy went up to visit Aunt Marian and Uncle Roy when he was fifteen years old because he loved the environment. He spent his summers at Aunt Marian and Uncle Roy's place for the next six years.

Some fifteen or twenty years later, I revisited the area. In the canyon the fir trees had grown to fifty to seventy-five feet and one couldn't tell where the canyon wall was. The little log cabin was still there, with a newer second cabin nearby. Later on, Randy went back and bought twenty square miles of land adjacent to where Aunt Marian and Uncle Roy used to live. Randy is now trying to sell the land that Aunt Marian and Uncle Roy owned.

Dead Sheep

When I was twelve, it was the first time my sister and I visited the cabin that Aunt and Uncle Weston had in the mountains, two miles north of Lava Hot Springs, Idaho which is sixty miles north of Utah. Their cabin was at the bottom of the canyon and there was a small stream of water.

It was just before the beginning of the evening. My uncle had gone up the canyon to bury a sheep that had died. He was about fifteen yards ahead of me. I had gone up the wall of the canyon to the top to look around and after I was walking back to the cabin. On the other side of the canyon there was a coyote that I was unaware of. As the sun began to go down the coyote began to howl but did come towards the cabin. I began running toward the cabin. Along the trek back to the cabin, there was a waterfall about twelve feet high dropping into a small creek. I kept running. I did not fall. I got to the cabin and laid down on the bed and rested. We went up to bury the sheep, with the coyote crying only fifteen feet away, at least that is what I thought (it was actually a half a mile). I was very tired and exhausted since I hadn't been up in the mountains that long. I had mountain sickness from excess activity, with a lot of retching and vomiting. My aunt and uncle just sat there laughing at me. I was a city boy who had become as miserable as could be, receiving no sympathy from them. The next time I went up to the canyon I didn't stay very long. From then on, whenever the sun was about to set, I made sure I was near the cabin.

Tree House

We lived in Oak Park, Illinois on a block where there were eight houses on one side of the alley and six houses on the other side of the alley. There were no houses on the west side. In part of that block, there was a fifty foot tall tree near the alley. A friend and I built a tree house in a branch about twelve feet above the ground. There were garden snakes in the tall wild grass. When I came back after my first year in college, my tree house was gone and there were no empty areas in the entire city. There were now houses everywhere and no tall trees.

When I was fifteen years old, I was permitted to drive a car. That year in the winter time, there was usually ice on the ground. There were streets, but no houses within a half a mile from where I lived. I would spin the car around at intersections. If the car started to skid, I automatically knew what to do. I don't think my parents knew about me spinning the car.

Ruth Velikovsky Sharon, PhD
My Second Wife

Ruth was born in Jerusalem in 1926, and arrived in the U.S. in 1939. She has been a resident of Princeton since 1955. She has a Bachelor's and Masters degrees from N.Y.U. and a Doctorate degree in Psychology from The Union Institute and University. We were married by Father Timothy at Saint Paul's Church in 2000. After a few months, we took a trip to Israel. We never traveled to Jerusalem since there was unrest in Israel and Ruth's niece, Raya, had just been killed by a bomb thrown into her kibbutz.

Ruth is the daughter of Immanuel Velikovsky, a well known psychiatrist and author of the book "Worlds in Collision", which in 1950, was only outsold by the Bible.

Her mother, Elis (Elisheva) Velikovsky, was a violinist and a sculptress. Her sculpture was chosen out of 5,000 submissions for an exhibit at the Metropolitan Museum of Art in 1951. It was in the first page of the catalogue.

Ruth co-authored a book with Marilu Henner titled, "I Refuse to Raise a Brat." And co-authored a book with me "The More You Explain the Less They Understand". She also wrote two books about her father, "Aba, The Glory and the Torment" and "The Truth Behind the Torment". She gifted her father's archives (which included Einstein and Freud letters) to Princeton University's Special Collections Library.

Being trained in art and in psychology, Ruth explained the similarity between the two professions: Namely, the analyst has to correctly anticipate the patient's reactions once speaking to the patient, and the artist has to be able to visualize the lines or colors before putting them on the canvas.

Father Timothy Capewell performing marriage vows at St Paul's church for John Cathro Seed MD and Ruth Velikovsky Sharon PhD on February 12, 2000

Following is a letter that Ruth sent to me after the passing of her mother (the letter was sent prior to when I married Ruth):

August 16, 1985

Dear Dr. Seed,

From the day my mother suffered a stroke on Labor Day 1982 until her death on June 23rd 1983 – with the exception of her six week stay at the Columbia Presbyterian Hospital (from approximately June 25th thru October 15th 1982) you were in charge of her case.

As she developed cancer and became depressed, you were competent, considerate, accessible, reliable, compassionate, steadfast, knowledgeable, cooperative, sensitive, accommodating, flexible, good humored, brilliant, hard working, devoted, caring, called in consultants, made daily house calls, sometimes twice and even three times in one day. You missed only one day because of a blizzard. You talked with my mother, cleared her nose, checked her blood pressure, and listened to her lungs and heart. You instructed us in walking her, taking her weight, feeding her, discussing her medication. You helped with the nurses and "helpers" and therapists who tended her.

Mrs. Seed was always friendly, professional, sympathetic and attentive whenever we called and we called endlessly – sometimes several times a day.

In conclusion – I have never in my life met a team like you and Mrs. Seed. You were the ones who made it possible to give my mother the kind of care I wanted her to have.

I have never written this type of letter containing adjectives to anyone. They are not written lightly. They are written sincerely – and it has been over two years since my mother's passing, so the gratitude to the doctors which fades soon after death will not and has not faded with me. In fact I recognize it more and more – and even on the early morning she died you voluntarily brought all her belongings including a cot that the private "helpers" slept on to our house.

Thank you –

Sincerely,

Ruth Velikovsky Sharon

Booksigning at Princeton University Bookstore

Nuts

Peanuts are dug out of the earth. Aflatoxin is a poisonous chemical that is made by a fungus that lives on the hulls of peanuts which causes cancer of the liver. The Food Drug Administration (FDA) has put a strict limit of the amount of aflatoxin that may be present in commercial peanut butter. However, there is no such limit for the peanut butter sold in health food stores. The FDA has no jurisdiction over their food because the stores grind the peanuts and make their own peanut butter.

Also, eating peanuts is the best way to cause hardening of the arteries and heart attacks in monkeys. Researchers, who study coronary artery disease in monkeys, feed them peanuts to cause coronary disease. If the monkeys eat their natural food, they do not get hardening of the arteries and heart attacks. Studies have not been done on the effects of peanuts on people, because nobody wants to design an experiment that causes people to die.

Eating peanuts are dangerous, but some nuts are beneficial. To demonstrate the beneficial effects of some nuts, a controlled study was done with walnuts. People were randomly assigned to one of two groups. One group had to eat thirty-five walnuts a day and the other group was forbidden to eat any nuts. The group eating walnuts had fewer heart attacks than those who did not. What made walnuts beneficial is gamma linolenic acid, an essential fatty acid that is required for making the myelin sheath around the nerves of the brain. Twelve percent of the fatty acids in walnuts are gamma linolenic and forty-six percent of the fatty acids in Brazil nuts are gamma linolenic. Brazil nuts and walnuts increase the amount of HDL (High Density Lipoprotein) in the blood. HDL cholesterol is the good cholesterol.

The high oleic content in pistachios makes them look good as a source of monounsaturated fat. But, pistachios are dry roasted, so the fat changes into a dangerous food. Walnuts and Brazil nuts are not roasted, so they increase the good HDL cholesterol. It is dangerous to roast any nuts.

Dieting and Smoking

How do you get a person to understand what a good diet is when a person is so resistant to it? Does a person have to have a heart attack in order to change his diet? In some people even a heart attack won't do it. They watch their diet for a few months after a heart attack, but within a year, they are back into the habit of eating eggs and bacon for breakfast. They must be thinking, "Well, I'll get my heart fixed and have another heart attack. I'll go see my doctor before I'm really having a heart attack and let him clear the artery!" What about a person who has high intelligence but won't check his cholesterol? They don't want to have their lifestyle interfered with, that's all. They know by going to see a doctor, well he's going to tell me I've got to stop smoking and stop having bacon for lunch and I don't want to. So, I'm not going to go to the doctor. I know what he's going to tell me and I don't want to hear that. What should I waste my money seeing a doctor and have him tell me something I don't want to do. If one wants to be like world famous athletes, then one shouldn't smoke. I've been a doctor for sixty years and have never gotten a girl to stop smoking. Yet, every single boy I've run into I've been able to stop smoking.

On Being Thirsty

Sometimes a person feels thirsty and drinks some water, but still feels thirsty. One can keep on drinking and the thirsty feeling never goes away but one is urinating frequently. What is happening is this: you are short on salt in the circulatory system. The volume of blood in the circulatory system is lower than it should be. The body needs water to make more blood but it also needs more salt. The circulatory system notifies the brain of the need for water, i.e., you feel thirsty, but there is no mechanism for notifying the brain of the need for salt. One of the jobs of the kidneys is to see to it that the salt concentration in the blood never gets too low. If the salt concentration in the body is at the low limit of normal and you drink water without salt, the water will just go out in your urine. The volume of the circulatory system will stay the same and you will still feel thirsty. If you drink some salty soup, the thirsty feeling will go away.

If one is working hard and sweating for a long time and not drinking any water while you are working, you will feel thirsty after a while. You will have lost volume from the circulatory system that is water but no salt. Now, if you drink water, it will stay in the body. The thirsty feeling will go away. But if you drink more than is needed, the kidney will put out the water in the urine.

Heel Spur

There is a tendon attached to each toe on the foot that combines into a single tendon attached to the heel. If an accident stresses the tendon severely enough that the damage might come at the heel, the foot will hurt when walking. If one puts pressure down on the heel at the site of the damage, it hurts. If you walk in your natural way, you are putting pressure on your heel. To avoid the pain one tends to walk on the toes. When one does this one is pulling the tendon away from the heel. In order to make the tendon firmly attached to the heel, the body builds a bone to the end of the tendon. It takes as much time to build the bone to the tendon as it does to build the bone to heal a fracture, i.e., four to six weeks. If one walks on the toes to lessen pain one is apt to pull the tendon loose from the bone. If this is done repeatedly one builds a boney spike from the heel out to the tendon. This is the heel spur.

One can prevent the spur from forming if you completely avoid putting pressure on the site of the damage. At the same time one would be speeding up the rate of healing. This means put an insert in the shoe that has in it a hole, over the place where pressure causes pain in that case enlarge the hole, and keep enlarging until there is no pain with pressure. Every time one walks around on the toes one would pull the heel away from the tendon and the bone building process starts over again which means another four to six weeks until it is healed. All the pressure should be on the edges of the bottom of the shoe.

Burning on Urination

When a woman gets a urinary infection, it is usually very painful to urinate. This is because the wall of the bladder is raw and inflamed and the urine is usually acidic. If you pour acid on a cut or open burn it hurts. One half a teaspoon of baking soda dissolved in water, prune juice, peach juice, etc. will change the urine from acidic to alkaline and urination will be comfortable while waiting for antibiotics to cure the infection.

Preventing Wound Odors

Wounds that have been open for weeks or months, e.g. cancer, sometimes generate an unpleasant odor. This odor can be prevented by washing the wound with ten percent lactose and then sprinkling the wound with the powder that is used for making yogurt. Lactose is the name for milk sugar. Lactose and yogurt powder can both be obtained over the internet. Ten percent is the concentration that is compatible with the tissues in the body. It is equivalent to the five percent glucose solution that is given intravenously. The powder for making yogurt changes lactose into lactic acid. Lactic acid is strong enough to precipitate milk protein into yogurt and will precipitate the proteins that the bacteria are living on and will kill most of the bacteria.

The Diagnosis of Streptococcal Sore Throat

Some beautiful, older data (1, 2) on the diagnosis of a streptococcal A sore throat seems to have been lost to modern medicine. The physicians at the Great Lakes Naval Station in Evanston, Illinois on the shores of Lake Michigan were seeing a lot of recruits with a sore throat in 1942 and wondered what the symptoms of a streptococcal sore throat really were. Any recruit coming into the infirmary with a sore throat had a careful history taken, a physical examination was done, and a blood sample was drawn to measure the antibodies to the streptolysin-O protein (ASO) that is contained in streptococcus A bacteria. The recruits had to come back daily for 10 days and their symptoms and physical findings were recorded at each visit. At their last visit, a blood sample was drawn for a second ASO titer. Those who had a rise in antibody titer of more than four fold were considered to have had a streptococcus A infection. In addition to a rise of in streptococcus there is a red color somewhere in the back of the throat. The surface of the membrane on the back of the throat appears in a bright red instead of a pink color and blood vessels are visible, this is because strep is a thick membrane from capillary blood vessels.

Potassium Chloride

Potassium chloride is available in supermarkets as a salt substitute; No salt and Nu Salt. Salt substitute has the most potassium chloride per gram of powder. A quarter of a teaspoon of salt substitute is all the potassium chloride that one needs for a day. However, it should not be swallowed as an undiluted powder. It can be put in a salt shaker designed to take only one quarter of a teaspoon of powder and then shaken out over potatoes and meat. Or alternatively, the salt can be dissolved in eight teaspoons of a liquid such as orange juice, prune juice, vegetable juice etc. <u>If the concentrated, undiluted potassium chloride is swallowed it could damage the wall of the esophagus, stomach, and intense. It is also dangerous to swallow a full teaspoon of potassium chloride at one time because it could stop the heart</u>. A container of salt substitute contains eighty-eight grams of powder, one half of which is potassium chloride and the other half consists of fumaric acid and some calcium phosphates to improve the flavor. There are seventy-four servings in a container and it costs $2.00 or about $0.03 per dose. There are tablets of potassium chloride containing the same amount of potassium chloride for up to $2.00 per tablet.

Curriculum Vitae
John C. Seed, M.D.

Born in 1922 at the Mayo Clinic in Rochester, Minnesota

Princeton University 1939-1942

Physical Chemistry major under Dr. Eyring - Partition Functions.
Five 1-year courses in college physics.
Four 1-year courses in college mathematics including statistics.
    No degree but Phi Beta Kappa.

Harvard Medical School 1942-1945

M. D. degree.
    Part-time, voluntary research in pharmacology under Drs. Krayer and Acheson.
    Worked on acetylcholine assays of corneal epithelium and the anticonvulsant action of
    veratrum viride.

Massachusetts General Hospital 1945-1946

Internship in internal medicine
    A fellow intern and I were the first to cure subacute bacterial endocarditis.
    Implemented a colorimetric method for determining blood hemoglobin levels.
    Isolated uroporphyrin III from a patient's urine.

Army Chemical Center, Medical Laboratories 1946-1950

Pharmacologist and physician in army uniform 1946-1949.
    Renal function studies, effects of nitrogen mustards on cell division, adrenergic block-
    ing agents, epinephrine assays.
    Clinical care of accidental poisonings.
    Assisted in writing the manual on the management of chemical warfare poisoning.
    Covering the station hospital nights and week ends along with the other 15 physicians
    in the group.
Chief, Aerosol Section as civilian 1949-1950.
    Section staff of 10 including 2 Ph.D.'s and 1 M.D.
    Classified work.

Sterling Winthrop Research Institute 1950-1954

(There were 470 employees at the Institute.)

Executive Assistant to the Director and Clinical Pharmacologist
Supervision of statistical work (I.B.M. punch card systems, data analysis, experimental. design).
Evaluation of screening procedures, pharmaceutical formulations, outside products, and preparation of technical exhibits and manuscripts.
Clinical trials of analgesics, laxatives, anti-epileptics, antispasmodics, and radiopaque drugs.

Burroughs Wellcome & Co. (U.S.A.) Inc., 1954-1962

Pharmacologist, clinical and laboratory
Clinical and laboratory studies of analgesic compounds, clinical dose-ranging studies, clinical trials of antifibrillatory compounds, consulting work on statistical analysis of data and design of experiments.
George Hitchings and Gertrude Elion who were recently awarded the Nobel Prize in medicine were associates of mine at Burroughs Wellcome.

Memorial Sloan-Kettering Cancer Center 1956-1967

Special Assignment in Anesthesiology.
Helped set up the pain program and conducted four experiments. Studies on the effects of narcotics on respiration.
Design and construction of a respiratory computer.

Calvary Hospital 1959-1965

(Located in the middle of the Bronx.)

Medical Director, Chief of Medical Service, Director of the Laboratory, Licensed as a Hospital Laboratory Director by the New York City Health Department.
Played a major role in converting a nursing home into a fully approved and accredited, 112-bed hospital for which I was awarded the **Pro Ecclesia et Pontifice by Pope John XXIII in 1962.** This is the highest award the church can bestow upon a layman. When first inspected by the Joint Commission on Accrediation of Hospitals they said that it was the best run hospital they had ever inspected.
Research on analgesics, antipyretics, cancer chemotherapy, kinetics of cell renewal in the intestinal tract, and a mathematical model for glucose homeostasis

Princeton University 1963- 1985

Visiting Lecturer and Research Associate in Electrical Engineering and Computer Science.
Computer simulation of appointment systems using SIMSCRIPT.

Design of efficient, flexible, data collecting and recording systems which minimize errors and computer programs for detecting data errors and automatically correcting them.

Special purpose programs for analysis of variance of drug trials, data reduction of anti-pyretic data and statistical analysis of data related to total body potassium content.

Design of medical information system for ambulatory care.

Computer programs for the management of colds and sore throats by the layman.

Since 1974, teaching a one semester course on Computer Applications in Medicine. For the three years before that a course on Medical Systems Analysis.

Faculty advisor for student independent work.

Pre-med advisor for engineering school students.

I worked at Princeton, Tuesday and Thursday afternoons and evenings. The rest of the week and Saturdays, I worked in the South Bronx, in the lowest per capita income and highest crime rate precinct in New York City.

Morrisania City Hospital 1965-1966

(Located in the South Bronx. Demolished in 1969.)
Director of Employee Health Service.
Emergency Room Physician.
Assistant Visiting Physician.

Cornell University Medical College 1965 - 1970

Visiting Lecturer in public health.
Teaching community health, computer programming and statistics.
Statistical and computer consulting in the Department of Medicine.

Martin Luther King Health Center 1966 - 1980

(Located in the South Bronx, employing 15 physicians and controlled by Montefiore Hospital.)

Family Physician.
Adjunct Attending Physician, Montefiore Hospital and Medical Center since 1968.
Patient care and training paramedical personnel.
Teaching family practice residents.
Director of Laboratories at the Martin Luther King Health enter 1968 - 1980.

Albert Einstein College of Medicine 1967- 1983

Instructor in Preventive Medicine and Community Health (Internist) in the Department of Social Medicine.

Fund for the City of New York 1974

Advisor on causes of building destruction, management of addiction and welfare problems.

System Development Foundation 1980 - 1986

(The Rand Corporation bought the System Development company for $100,000,000 all of which went to the Foundation which spent it on supporting work on neurobiology and artificial intelligence.)

Consultant.
Traveled to sites requesting funds and sites funded by the Foundation to interview the people and evaluate their work.

Solo, Private Practice. Princeton. NJ 1980 - present

Medical Center at Princeton
Associate Attending   1980   -   1982
Attending Physician   1982   -   2002
Senior Attending   2002   -   present
Instructor for students of UMDNJ-Robert Wood Johnson Medical School 1981 - 1993
Physical Diagnosis Course. Offered at Medical Center at Princeton.
Chairman, Department of Family Practice 1983 - 1996
Member, Physicians Advisory Committee to Information Systems Department 1990 - present
The Information Systems Department manages the hospital's computer system. Other Committee Memberships: Pharmacy, By-Laws, Radiation Safety

Princeton Individual Practice Association. 1982 - 2002

Co-Founder
Member of the Board of Trustees 1982 - 2002
Secretary of the Board of Trustees 1982 - 2002

HeartCare Partners 1999 - 2001

(This was a firm being developed in collaboration with one of my sons who is a full professor of molecular biology at Harvard Medical School. It was devoted to clearing out hardening of arteries by medical means only, using some methods that I had developed.)
President

Publications
John C. Seed, M.D.

1. Seed, J.C.
   Veratrum Viride, Boylston Essays, Harvard Medical School, 1945

2. Sweet, W. H., Cotzias, G. C., Seed, J. C., Yakovlev, P.
   Gastrointestinal Hemorrhages, Hyperglycemia, Azotemia, Hyperchloremia and Hypernatremia Following Lesions of the Frontal Lobes in Man.
   Assoc, Res. Nervous and Mental Diseases 27:795, 1947.

3. Kennedy, B. J., Seed, J. C.
   The Treatment of Subacute Bacterial Endocarditis with Penicillin in Beeswax Oil.
   Am. Heart J. 34:906, 1947

4. Seed, J. C., McKay, E.
   Effect of 933E on the Action of Dibenamine.
   Fed. Proc. 8:143, 1949

5. Seed, J. C., McKay, E.
   Inhibition by Piperidinomethyl-3-benzodioxane of Epinephrine Vasopressor Blockade Produced by Dibenzyl-g-chlorethylamine.
   Proc. Soc. Exp. Biol. Med: 70:724, 1949.

6. Calkins, E., Dana, G. W., Seed, J. C., Howard, J. E.
   Piperidomethylbenzodioxane: Some Pharmacological and Experimental Observations.
   J. Clin. Endocrin. 9:651, 1949

7. Landing, B. H., Seed, J. C., Banfield, W.
   The Effects of a Nitrogen Mustard (Tris 2-chlorethylamine) on Regenerating Rat Liver.
   Cancer 2:1067, 1949

8. Seed, J. C., Wilson, C. E.
   Fluorimetric Determination of Serum Aureomycin Levels.
   Sci. 110:707, 1949

9. Calkins, E., Dana, G. W., Seed, J. C., Howard, J. E.
   On Piperidomethylbensodioxane, Hypertension and Pheochromocytoma. J. Clin.
   Endocrin. 10:1, 1950

174

10. Seed, J. C., Wilson, C. E.
   Effect of Aluminum Hydroxide on Serum Aureomycin Concentrations after Simultaneous Oral Administration.
   Bull. Johns Hopkins Hosp. 86:415, 1950

11. Dill, D. B. , Seed, J. C., Marxulli, F. N.
   Energy Expenditure in Bicycle Riding.
   Am. J. Physiol. 163:708, 1950

12. Seed, J. C., Harris, R.
   Some Factors in the Design of Aperient Studies.
   Ann. N.Y. Acad. Sci. 58:426, 1954

13. Coulston, F., Seed, J. C.
   The Relationship of Psyllium Seed and Various Fractions of the Seed to Kidney Pigmentation.
   J. Am. Pharm. Assoc. Sci. Ed. 45:716, 1956

14. Steinberg, S. S., Bellville, J. W., Seed, J. C.
   The Effect of Atropine and Morphine on Respiration.
   J. Pharm. Exp. Therap. 121:71, 1957

15. Bellville, J. W., Seed, J. C.
   Servomechanisms in Pharmacology.
   Fed. Proc. 17:1374, 1958

16. Seed, J. C., Wallenstein, S. L., Houde, R. W., and Bellville, W. A.
   Comparison of the Analgesic and Respiratory Effects of Dihydrocodeine and Morphine in Man.
   Arch. int. pharmacodyn. 116:293, 1958

17. Seed, J. C., Acton, F. S., Stunkard, A. J.
   A system for Glucose Metabolism.
   J. Clin. Invest. 37:930, 1958

18. Bellville, J. W., Seed, J. C.
   Respiratory Carbon Dioxide Response Curve Computer. Sci. 130:1079, 1959

19. Bellville, J. W., Seed, J. C.
   The Use of an Analogue Computer for Measurement of Respiratory Depression.
   Trans. N.Y. Acad. Sci. Ser. II, Vol. 22:34, 1959

20. Bellville, J. W., Howland, W. S., Seed, J. C., Houde, R. W.
   The Effect of Sleep on the Respiratory Response to Carbon Dioxide.
   Anesthesiology 20:628, 1959

21. Bellville, J. W., Seed, J. C.
   The Effect of Drugs on the Respiratory Responses to Carbon Dioxide.
   Anesthesiology 21:727, 1960

22. Seed, J. C., Acton, F. S., Stunkard, A. J.
     A Model for the Appraisal of Glucose Metabolism.
     Clin. Pharm. Therap. 3:191, 1962

23. Seed, J. C.
     A Clinical Comparison of the Antipyretic Potency of Aspirin and Sodium Salicy-
     late.
     Clin. Pharm. Therap. 6:354, 1965

24. Seed, J. C., Acton, F. S.
     Clinical Trials of Antipyretic Drugs.
     Chapter 16, pp 297-308 in Clinical Pharmacology, edited by L. Lasagna.
     Volume 1 of Section 6 of International-Encyclopedia of Pharmacology and
     Therapeutics, Pergamon Press, London and New York, 1966

25. Bellville, J. W., Seed, J. C.
     A Comparison of the Respiratory Depressant Effects of Dextropropoxyphene
     and Codeine in Man.
     Clin. Pharm. Therap. 9:428, 1968

26. Seed, J. C.
     The Value of Medical Information.
     Third Annual Symposium on Information Sciences, Princeton. pp. 298-302

27. Seed, J. C.
     Some Objectives for Therapeutic and Drug Prescribing Aspects of a Computer
     System for Ambulatory Medical Care.
     Am. J. Hosp. Pharm. 26:436, 1969

28. Seed, J. C.
     Restricted Data Formats.
     Ann. N.Y. Acad. Sci. 161:484, 1969

The More You Explain ...
The Less They Understand

Ruth Velikovsky Sharon, Ph.D.
John Cathro Seed, M.D.

ISBN 978-1-906833-00-8

In this, perhaps the most encompassing of her works, Dr. Ruth Velikovsky Sharon brilliantly lifts the veil that shrouds the mystery of psychoanalysis, revealing intrinsic truths that can forever assist us in our journey to self-discovery and growth.

Like a finely tuned and well-trained instrument, Dr. Sharon makes her probe into the human psyche sound easy – resulting in a compilation of luminous insights that are warm in their humanity, vibrant in their simplicity, and even touched with humor.

Harvard Medical School Graduate, Dr. John C. Seed's contribution of the Physical Health chapter will enlighten the medical community as well as the average reader, and if abided by, will help prolong life.

Shame on You –
You Were in My Dream

Ruth Velikovsky Sharon, Ph.D.

ISBN 978-1-906833-01-5

Finally a new and easy guide to the understanding of dreams, which really makes sense!

Ruth Velikovsky Sharon, PhD has developed a completely new understanding of the nature of dreams, which is fascinating because of its simplicity and its practical orientation.

She questions ideas we have long taken for granted. She asks us to reconsider what the word "dream" really means. She shows us that to use the word "dream" in partnership with "He is a dreamboat" or "My dream house!" is to misuse or even abuse the word "dream".

In her book, Dr. Sharon describes the way that parents can be of help vis a vis dreams: Listen and Learn. Ask your children how they felt in the dream, ask them what they thought in the dream. She includes chapters on manipulation in dreams, dream catchers and other gadgets and the environment and dreams.

Also included is a reprint of the article »A New Understanding of Dreams«, published by Dr. Sharon in *New Jersey Medicine*, Journal of the Medical Society of New Jersey, January 1995 issue.

ABA – The Glory
and the Torment

Ruth Velikovsky Sharon, Ph.D.

ISBN 978-1-906833-20-6

In this book you get to know Immanuel Velikovsky as a person. His daughter Ruth describes his childhood, his family environment and his eventful life.

Using plenty of background information, numerous anecdotes and many photographs she makes us familiar with her father, but also shows the personal dimension of the devastating campaign he encountered in the last decades of his life.

The Truth
Behind the Torment

Ruth Velikovsky Sharon, Ph.D.

ISBN 978-1-906833-21-3

In this supplement to her father's biography, Ruth Velikovsky Sharon, Ph.D. depicts the true facts about the campaign against him.

She publishes revealing letters in full length, that show the true nature of the undeserving – unscientific – treatment of Velikovsky by the scientific establishment, a treatment that appears rather medieval than enlightened.

Also included is a chapter written by plasma physicist C. J. Ransom, Ph.D. dealing with Velikovsky's theories and the controversy about our Solar System, the ancient sky and the role of electromagnetism in cosmology.

Imagine Art

Works of Art by
Ruth Velikovsky Sharon, Ph.D.
and Elisheva Velikovsky

ISBN 978-1-906833-02-2

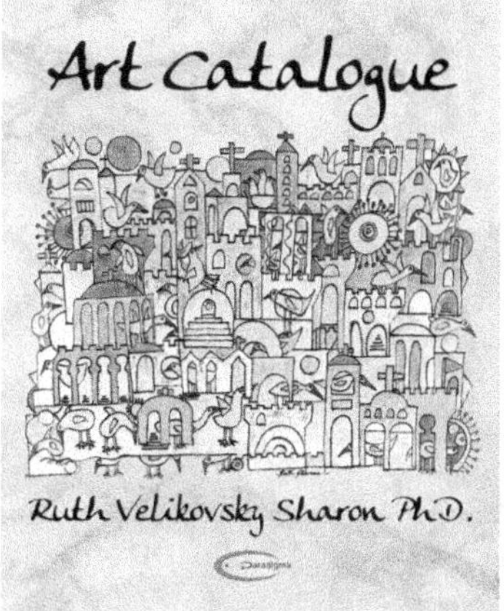

Art Catalogue

Ruth Velikovsky Sharon, Ph.D.

ISBN 978-1-906833-03-9

The name of Velikovsky is mainly known from the scientific and historical discoveries of Immanuel Velikovsky.

Far less known is the artistic dimension in the Velikovsky family, mainly expressed by Elisheva (or "Elis") Velikovsky and Ruth Velikovsky Sharon, PhD., the wife and daughter of Immanuel Velikovsky. For everyone interested in and fond of visual and plastic arts these booklets will give an exhaustive overview of the remarkable range of the works of these two artists.

Worlds in Collision

Immanuel Velikovsky

ISBN 978-1-906833-11-4

With this book Immanuel Velikovsky first presented the revolutionary results of his 10-year-long interdisciplinary research to the public – and caused an uproar that is still going on today.

Worlds in Collision – written in a brilliant, easily understandable and entertaining style and full to the brim with precise information – can be considered one of the most important and most challenging books in the history of science. Not without reason was this book found open on Einstein's desk after his death.

For all those who have ever wondered about the evolution of the earth, the history of mankind, traditions, religions, mythology or just the world as it is today, *Worlds in Collision* is an absolute MUST-READ!

Earth in Upheaval

Immanuel Velikovsky

ISBN 978-1-906833-12-1

After the publication of *Worlds in Collision* Immanuel Velikovsky was confronted with the argument that in the shape of the earth and in the flora and fauna there are no traces of the natural catastrophes he had described.

Therefore a few years later he published *Earth in Upheaval* which not only supports the historical documents by very impressive geological and paleontological material, but even arrives at the same conclusions just based on the testimony of stones and bones.

Earth in Upheaval – a very exactly investigated and easily understandable book – contains material that completely revolutionizes our view of the history of the earth.

For all those who have ever wondered about the evolution of the earth, the formation of mountains and oceans, the origin of coal or fossils, the question of the ice ages and the history of animal and plant species, *Earth in Upheaval* is a MUST-READ!

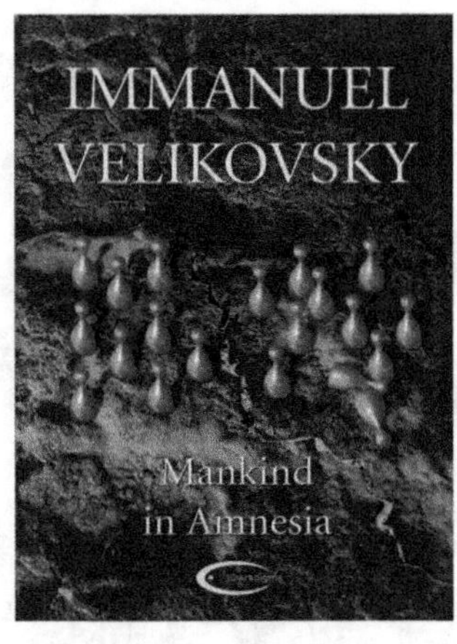

Mankind in Amnesia

Immanuel Velikovsky

ISBN 978-1-906833-16-9

Immanuel Velikovsky called this book the "fulfillment of his oath of Hippocrates – to serve humanity." In this book he returns to his roots as a psychologist and psychoanalytical therapist, yet not with a single person as his patient but with humanity as a whole.

After an extremely revealing overview of the foundations of the various psychoanalytical systems he makes the step into crowd psychology and reopens the case of *Worlds in Collision* from a totally different point of view: as a psychoanalytical case study. In this way he shows that the blatant reactions to his theories (which are still going on today) have not been surprising but actually inevitable from a psychological perspective – which equally holds for those who have defined our view of the world. At the same time he is able to reclassify the theories of Siegmund Freud and of C. G. Jung finding a common basis for them.

A journey through history, religion, mythology and art shows the overall range of the collective trauma and gives us – the patients – a message of extraordinary urgency and importance for the future.

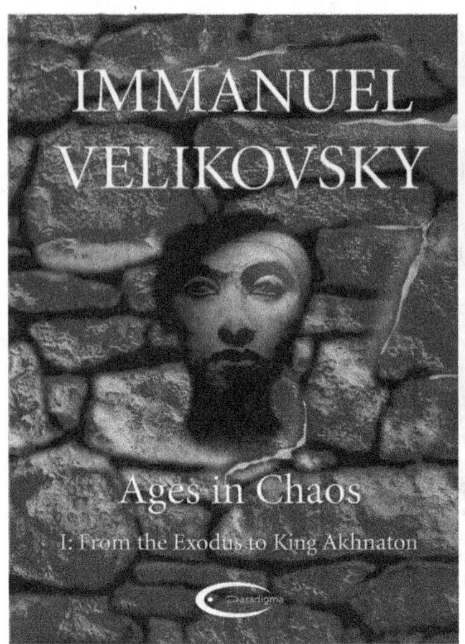
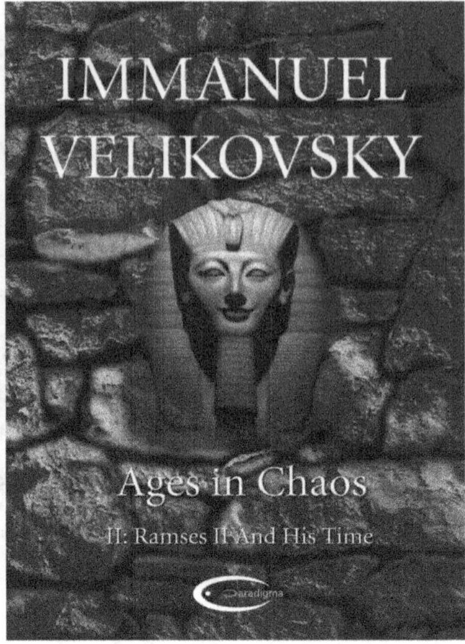
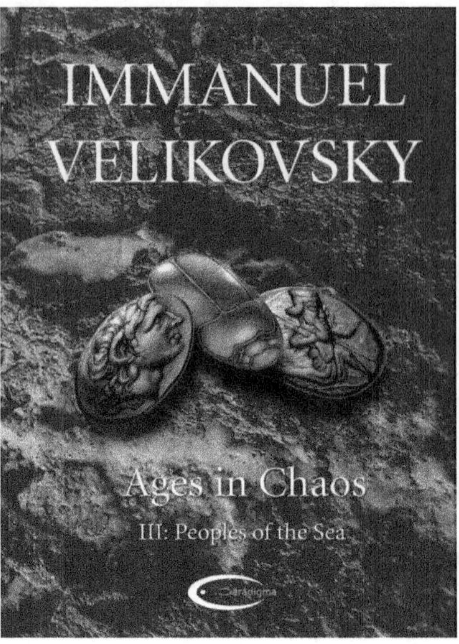

Ages in Chaos

Immanuel Velikovsky

I: From the Exodus to King Akhnaton	II: Ramses II and His Time	III: Peoples of the Sea
ISBN 978-1-906833-13-8	ISBN 978-1-906833-14-5	ISBN 978-1-906833-15-2

In his series *Ages in Chaos*, Immanuel Velikovsky undertakes a reconstruction of the history of antiquity.

With utmost precision and the exciting style of presentation typical for him he shows beyond any doubt what nobody would consider possible: in the conventional history of Egypt – and therefore also of many neighboring cultures – a span of more than 600 years is described which has never happened! This assertion is as unbelievable and outrageous as the assertions in *Worlds in Collision* or *Earth in Upheaval*. But Velikovsky takes us on a detailed and highly interesting journey through the – corrected – history and makes us witness, how many question marks disappear, doubts vanish and corresponding facts from the entire Near East furnish a picture of overall conformity and correctness. In the end you not only wonder how conventional historiography has come into existence, but why it is still taught and published.

In an extensive supplement to *Peoples of the Sea* Velikovsky delves into the fundamental question of how such a dramatic shift in chronology could have come about.

In a further supplement he discusses the very interesting conclusions that can be drawn from radiocarbon testing on Egyptian archeological finds.

Just as Velikovsky became the father of "neo-catastrophism" by *Worlds in Collision*, he became the father of "new chronology" by *Ages in Chaos*.